STYLE & SPEED

STYLE & SPEED

The World's Greatest Sports Cars

ROB LEICESTER WAGNER

MetroBooks

An Imprint of Friedman/Fairfax Publishers

Library of Congress Cataloging-in-Publication Data

Wagner, Rob, 1954-
    Style and speed : the world's greatest sports cars / Rob Leicester
Wagner.
        p.   cm.
        Includes bibliographical references (p.).
        ISBN 1-56799-633-7
        1. Sports cars. I. Title.
TL236.W24   1998
629.228—dc21   98-18918

Editor: Ann Kirby
Art Director: Kevin Ullrich
Art Designer: Jonathan Gaines
Photography Editor: Wendy Missan
Production Manager: Susan Kowal

Color separations by HK Scanner Arts Int'l Ltd.
Produced by Phoenix Offset / Printed in China

1 3 5 7 9 10 8 6 4 2

For bulk purchases and special sales, please contact:
Friedman/Fairfax Publishers
Attention: Sales Department
15 West 26th Street
New York, NY 10010
212/685-6610 FAX 212/685-1307

Visit our website:
http://www.metrobooks.com

DEDICATION

For Deniece

ACKNOWLEDGMENTS

Special thanks to Hans Nohr and Eric Grunden of Absolutely British auto restorers in Ontario,
California, for their expertise on Austin-Healeys, MGs, and Triumphs, and to Richard Gray,
colleague and Porsche enthusiast, for his contributions on Porsches. Grateful appreciation also is
extended to the dozens of sports car owners in the Los Angeles area
who patiently discussed their unique collections with me.

CONTENTS

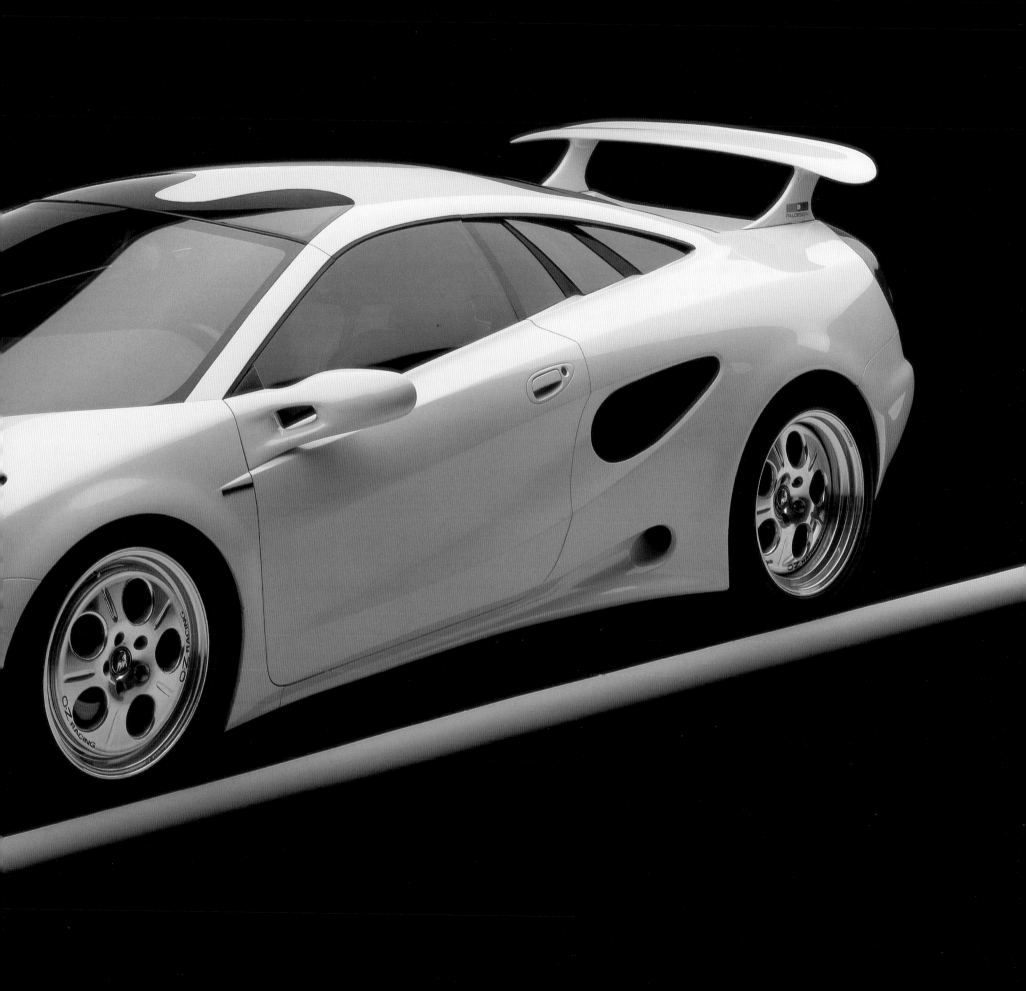

INTRODUCTION

There was a time in the not-so-distant past when people drove cars and not the other way around. Anti-lock braking systems, electronically controlled suspension and transmission systems, and computerized sensors have conspired to take the responsibility of driving out of our hands.

Ironically, the race car has helped lead us to this sorry state. Though not responsible for many of the inventions we now enjoy in production cars, the racing profession has helped to advance automotive technology. Lightweight engines and chassis, composite materials for lightweight bodies, the electronic ignition, double overhead cams, rack and pinion steering, oil coolers, and the like were all perfected on race cars before becoming standard equipment on production vehicles.

With these comforts we lose the thrill of driving. But the road to ultracomfortable driving is lined with an extraordinary evolution of vehicles. Sports cars heightened the driver's relationship with the road and his machine to an almost erotic level. We can thank postwar Europe for the ride.

Americans have always rested at the bottom of the sports car food chain. In spite of the Indianapolis 500, and even with such racing greats as Dan Gurney and Bob Bondurant on the United States' roster, American race cars and race car drivers never achieved the kind of greatness exemplified by Mike Hawthorn, Stirling Moss, or Juan Manuel Fangio. American drivers appear to lack the sensual passion of European drivers, who routinely take their machines to the edge and, instead of pulling back, push them a bit further to test the limits.

Organized endurance race car driving began in Europe after World War II, and followed in short order in the United States. The difference between the European and the American approach to racing was deeply affected by the war, and warrants some attention. Americans in the twentieth century were never faced with an enemy invading their borders; they never fought house to house, street corner to street corner to protect their families. They were never faced with the prospect of losing their families, their homes, and their property in an instant to an invading army. The psychological effect of war on England, Germany, and Italy had far-reaching implications that included racing sports.

Auto racing doesn't sound like logical fallout from war-ravaged Europe. Still, it's no coincidence that auto racing began almost the instant that Nazi Germany surrendered. It was an inexpensive distraction to the hunger, grief, and loss that Europeans were experiencing. Race driving was an extremely dangerous business in the late 1940s and 1950s, with drivers who were competing at breakneck speeds, often in inferior, prewar cars. There were no rollbars, inadequate helmets, poor tire technology, and few safety regulations. But these dangers paled in comparison to the horrors of war that many Europeans had so recently experienced. So speed records were established at a stunning pace, each event eclipsing the previous record.

The casual American observer during this period could little appreciate the European approach to racing. American race fans were brought up on big and fat—if not gaudy—American cars. Detroit told the people what was stylish and what should be bought. Gasoline, for crying out loud, cost less than 20 cents per gallon (3.7L). While Detroit emphasized styling and design, American automotive technology was stunted at prewar levels, as automakers focused on styling instead of mechanics.

With the incredible achievements of European racing, such as advancements in design and engine performance and increased speed, automotive technology improved. Soon, Sunday motorists were demanding that the same technology—the same engines that powered Jaguars, Ferraris, and Triumphs—be made available to them. Thus, the production sports car was born. On a more modest level, production sports car owners could experience nearly the same thrills as their factory race car–driving counterparts.

The English in particular experienced a renaissance in early postwar sports car driving. With more disposable income than the war-weary Germans and Italians, the English market was ready for new options, and introduced the MG, Triumph, Aston Martin, and Jensen, among others.

Stirling Moss, in a Vanwall identified as No. 18 at the far right, starts the European Grand Prix at Aintree in England on July 21, 1957. Moss captured first place with an average speed of 86.8 mph (139.7 kph) after No. 18 died in the pits and he took over another Vanwall.

But in Germany and Italy, which had come up on the losing end in the war, people were virtually impoverished, with less opportunities to purchase and drive sports cars. Perhaps it was because the Germans and Italians were a little hungrier than the English that they created the best sports cars ever, and won bucketfuls of racing victories.

This book pays homage to some of the best sports cars ever produced. After reviewing the histories of the finest automobiles ever built, I chose fourteen marques that I feel stand out as the world's greatest sports cars in terms of technology, racing prowess, and even marketing. MG, for example, may never be considered one of the fastest race cars of all time, but its sexy, old-style design and the nostalgia it inspired in American servicemen was a marketing coup, even if it was an accident.

With any discussion of the greatest sports cars comes the inevitable disclaimers. This book covers at length the specifications of many cars, and is limited to production sports cars only unless otherwise noted. Often—particularly with luxury sports cars like Ferrari, Maserati, and Lamborghini—specifications change from model to model, sometimes even car to car within the same production run.

In other instances, the automaker didn't release specifications. Specifications noted in this text have been gleaned from multiple sources, and when sources differed, I turned to the Standard Catalog of Imported Cars, 1946–1990 as the final word.

There are some sports cars that didn't make the final cut. Mercedes-Benz, for example, captured many victories on the racing circuit in the 1950s, but it wasn't primarily a sports car manufacturer. One of my personal favorites, Morgan, also is absent. On the other hand, I've included MG and Triumph, neither of which achieved great success on the race circuit. However, these two marques both deserve attention because of their impact on the U.S. market. They essentially introduced Americans to sports car driving.

As automotive technology improved and restrictive U.S. safety and emissions regulations were introduced, many sports car owners struggled to find the perfect car that would marry speed and road handling. Toward the end of the 1970s, styling became sharper and more angled, and with these changes some of the romanticism was lost.

Automakers recognized the growing void. The return to open-air roadsters came from a surprising source: in the

The 1998 Porsche Boxster shows that Porsche is just as innovative now as it was in the 1950s, with classic styling and excellent road handling.

summer of 1989, Mazda introduced the MX-5 Miata, a retro-style roadster based on the handsome styling of the 1960s Lotus Elan. The Miata not only sparked renewed interest among sports car enthusiasts, it attracted a new generation of buyers who hungered for a car that resembled the old-style roadsters but was still affordable at under $14,000.

The luxury carmakers soon followed. In 1997, Jaguar came out with its new XJ8, which recalled the styling of the XKE, and Porsche debuted its Boxster, drawing on some characteristics of the Type 356. Corvette and BMW also offered their own versions of retro styling.

It's fitting that at the end of the century—nearly fifty years after the founding of Grand Prix racing and the glamour of 1950s road racing—European and American automakers are drawing on the past to celebrate the renewed vigor in sports motoring.

CHAPTER ONE

AC COBRA

The AC Cobra was built on the concept of stuffing a huge, American-made V8 engine into a short, lightweight frame, then driving it like a bat out of hell.

This hybrid couldn't have been possible without a heavy dose of British workmanship in the form of AC Cars. AC—Auto Carrier—was founded in 1908 and began producing two-seater sports cars, powered by L-head 1496-cc engines, in 1920. Two-liter, 6-cylinder Bristol engines were introduced two years later.

After World War II, the company put out a line of modest cars, including a 2-liter sports saloon and a drophead coupe. By 1953, AC owners Charles and Derek Hurlock returned to the sports car game by bringing in designer John Tojeiro to develop the highly regarded AC Ace two-seater sports car. Built at the company's plant in Thames Ditton, Surrey, the Ace was the father of the Shelby Cobra in appearance. It was constructed with 3-inch (7.6cm) -diameter tubes for the chassis and independent wishbone and leaf spring suspension at the four corners. The wheelbase measured only 90 inches (228.6cm), with an overall length of 151.5 inches (384.8cm) and a mere height of 49 inches (124.4cm). It was an amazingly light machine at 1,685 pounds (764.9kg). The 6-cylinder engine, however, was modest at best with a 2-liter displacement to generate 85 horsepower at 4500 rpm. Still, the Ace could go from 0 to 60 mph (96.5kph) in a respectable 11.4 seconds.

Production of these sports cars was limited to a couple of hundred, but AC followed up in 1958 with the Aceca two-seater fastback coupe.

By the end of 1960, Carroll Shelby, a Texas racing enthusiast with a bad heart, was finishing out his career getting pasted by his competitors at the Riverside (California) Raceway in his 3-liter Maserati. He was calling it quits, but he was already dreaming of producing a lightweight sports car with a tough chassis and powered by an engine big enough to stand your hair on end in the curves.

Shelby began looking around for the chassis and body that would fulfill his dream. He determined that the AC's Ace chassis would fit the bill. AC, meanwhile, was seeing its supply of Bristol engines dwindle and was not planning to obtain new ones. AC was happy to oblige Shelby with a steady supply of Ace chassis. The Hurlocks were so enamored of giving their beloved Ace a new life that they even shipped the

The Ace-Bristol, the father of the Shelby Cobra, was a no-nonsense, even brutal machine. It was capable of hitting 60 mph (96.5 kph) in 9.1 seconds and a quarter-mile in 16 seconds with its 1971-cc engine with a braking horsepower of 105 at 4750 rpm. The Ace-Bristol engine was based on the 1930s BMW six. This is the 1956 version.

parts to Shelby in the United States on credit, based on Shelby's good name. The entire car sans engine and transmission was built at the Surrey plant, then shipped to Shelby-American, Inc., in Venice, California. The first car arrived in February 1962.

Shelby stiffened the frame and installed disc brakes to replace the Ace drums. He also flared the wheelwells to accommodate larger tires. He had tinkered with the thought of putting a Chevrolet or Buick V8 in his new toy, but General Motors balked at the idea of being part of a sports car that would compete against its Corvette. That left Ford to pick up the challenge. It offered Shelby a lightweight cast-iron Fairlane 260-cubic-inch V8. Shelby brought in designer Pete Brock to strengthen and slightly alter the AC chassis to accommodate the powerplant. An optional 289-cubic-inch V8 came later.

This aluminum-bodied car was all brute strength with a major attitude and little finesse, and was awfully squirrelly on curves. It was not a sports car that allowed the driver to open the throttle on a curve. Top speeds could hit 136 mph (218.8kph) with a breathtaking 0–60 mph (0–96.5kph) in less than 5.5 seconds. This was with the 289 V8, which offered 271 braking horsepower but was capable of as much as 350 braking horsepower with race tuning.

In October 1962, the Cobra entered its first race with Bill Krause driving No. 0002 in a 3-hour preliminary run at the 1962 Times Grand Prix. Krause quickly hammered a Corvette—which would become Cobra's nemesis—early in the race, but fell out with a broken rear hub.

Cobras drew wide attention for high speeds the following February, but broke down at both the Daytona and Sebring races. That didn't stop Shelby, who continued to jerry-build the cars back together and put them on the track again. After their first year in existence, Cobras evolved into very dependable machines. They weren't pretty, with Shelby's Band-Aid approach to repairs, but they began finishing races.

During the 1963 season, two Cobras were entered at Le Mans, with one finishing seventh overall and fourth in the GT category behind three successive Ferrari GTOs.

By 1964, the Daytona coupe made its entrance into the racing field. Built for the long distance races at Daytona, Sebring, and Le Mans, the Daytona was designed to be competitive at speeds of up to 175–200 mph (281.5–321.8kph). Emphasis was on driver comfort, chassis strength, and aerodynamics—hence the coupe. Designer Pete Brock worked again with Shelby on the project to develop the styling, while chief engineer Phil Remington focused his attention on a redesigned chassis. Competition director Ken Miles worked on the interior for driver comfort.

In February 1964, exactly a year after several frustrating experiences with breakdowns in the other Shelby-American cars, the Daytona coupe entered the Daytona Continental 1,000km race. After completing 200 laps in the 327-lap race, it held a commanding 3-lap lead over the second-place car. But as the race drew to a close, the coupe overheated and caught fire in the pits.

But the Daytona effort served as only a warm-up for the 12-hour Sebring marathon race. This time, Bob Holbert and Dave MacDonald combined to lead the Daytona coupe to a 1-2-3 Cobra win in the GT class and fourth overall behind three Ferraris. Later in the '64 season, drivers Dan Gurney and Bob Bondurant led the Daytona coupe to a fourth-place finish at Le Mans.

The Daytona coupe was never intended for street use, and only six of them were ever produced.

Low slung with a wide, gaping, mouth-like grille, the Cobra, like this 1965 model, often outfoxed its nemesis, the Corvette. A series of American races in the early and mid-1960s cemented Cobra's dominance over its toughest rival, Corvette.

In all, seventy-five 260-cubic-inch V8 Cobras and fifty-one 289s were produced. Initially, the new product was named the AC Ford Cobra, then AC Cobra, and then just plain Cobra. By 1964, Shelby installed Ford's monstrous 427 into a wider and stronger chassis with the wheelbase lengthened from 90 to 96 inches (228.6 to 243.8cm) and 4-inch (10.1cm) tubes instead of the 3-inchers (7.6cm). The new dimensions gave the Cobra a more muscular look and eliminated the stress fractures found under the doors in the 3-inch (7.6cm) -tube versions.

The comfort level was kept to a minimum. The 427 was a car that was best driven in short distances. Engine heat seeped into the cockpit, making long afternoon drives during the summer almost unbearable. The convertible top was likened by many owners to a tent wrapped around a rather uncooperative collapsible frame. The lack of roll-up windows made the driver and passenger vulnerable to poor weather conditions.

Such distractions are a minor price to pay for the thrill of unadulterated power rumbling at your feet and screaming when the accelerator is punched to the floor.

Like a supernova, the Cobra experienced a brief but startling life span of just four years. It was a remarkable machine that today commands six-figure prices and a strong constitution from its driver. Shelby went on to produce the nearly equally spectacular Shelby Mustangs, while AC produced a British version of the Cobra called the AC 428 with the Ford Interceptor V8 instead of the 427. AC offered a convertible and a fastback coupe through 1973.

AC Cobra 427 (1965)

SPECIFICATIONS

Weight — 2,529 lbs. (1,148.2kg)

Tire size — 8.15x15

Engine type — Overhead-valve V8

Bore and stroke — 4.24x3.7 in.

Displacement — 427 cu. in. (6997 cc)

Compression ratio — 10.5:1

Carburetor — 2 Holley 4-barrel carburetors

Braking horsepower — 355 @ 5400 rpm

Transmission — 4-speed manual

DIMENSIONS

Wheelbase — 90 in. (228.6cm)

Length — 156 in. (396.2cm)

Height — 51 in. (129.5cm)

Width — 67 in. (170.1cm)

Front tread — 56 in. (142.2cm)

Rear tread — 56 in. (142.2cm)

PERFORMANCE

0–60 mph (0–96.5kph) — 4.3 seconds

Quarter mile (402.3m) — 12.2 seconds

Top speed — 162 mph (260.6kph)

CARROLL SHELBY

Cadillacs, either; he also found Mercury, Ford, and Chrysler engines equally effective.

Allard's creation must have had a profound influence on Carroll Shelby, a chicken farmer with a penchant for Texas chili who tore up dusty southern racetracks with wins in a Cad-Allard. When Shelby dreamed up the brilliant and monstrous AC Cobra in late 1961, he no doubt drew on his experience with the Allard as somewhat of a blueprint.

Wearing striped bib overalls and a cowboy hat and talking with a deliberate Texas twang, Carroll Shelby is the antithesis of a romantic race car driver. No, he wasn't the American version of a Peter Collins or a Juan Manuel Fangio. Rather, Shelby was the genuine article in auto racing: a man totally comfortable with himself and the world around him, whether it was on a track in Norman, Oklahoma, or in Paris. And it was Carroll Shelby who put American race drivers on the world map of auto racing with cars created by Shelby-American of Venice, California.

Carroll Hall Shelby was born on January 11, 1923, to Warren Hall and Eloise Lawrence Shelby in the tiny east Texas town of Leesburg. As a child he often sat in the shade and watched his father, the town postmaster, tinker with the family's 1925 Overland touring car. It was his first exposure to automobiles and led to his lifelong obsession. His experience with racing was pretty much limited to illegal street drags as a teenager, but

World War II put a stop to any thoughts of a career on the track.

In November 1941, he joined the Air Corps and was stationed at Lackland Air Force Base near San Antonio, Texas. Serving as a flight instructor, he remained stateside throughout the war. Two years later, he married Jeanne Fields and they had three children in quick succession: Sharon in '44, Michael in '46, and Patrick in '47. After Shelby's discharge from the service, his days were occupied as a roustabout, owning and operating dump trucks, then helping to build a portion of Route 66 near McLean, then roughnecking in the oil fields. Raising money to feed his wife and three children was his priority. Racing dropped a few notches down the list.

That changed in 1949 when he went into the poultry business and earned a clean $5,000 profit. His next batch of chickens, however, contracted Limberneck disease and wiped him out. For Shelby, it was time for a career change. "I decided that if I was going to go broke, it might as well be at something I like to do," he recalled.

Less than three years later he found himself on a quarter-mile (402.3m) drag strip behind the wheel of a hot rod powered by a flathead Ford V8. In May 1952, he drove in his first true race at Norman, Oklahoma, capturing first place in an MG-TC against a field of other MGs. The same day, he borrowed a Jaguar XK 120 from a friend to engage in a stiffer race and won again. He drove his first Cad-Allard late in the year in an early Sports Car Club of America (SCCA) race at Cadd Mills, Texas.

Still working the farm during those early years, Shelby had to drive from home to Fort Worth to compete in the race, and he didn't have enough time to change into his racing duds. He showed up at the track wearing striped bib overalls. He took second place

For many Europeans in the late 1940s the mere idea of shoehorning a brutish, unrefined American powerplant into a delicate, finely crafted featherweight British or Italian chassis was practically immoral. What did the makers of those sluggish behemoths in Detroit know about massive torque at high revs? Mixing European technology with American ingenuity was akin to attending a cockfight and not expecting to be splashed with a little blood.

This isn't to say that wedging Detroit iron onto a European frame was entirely unheard of. The British had tinkered with the idea, and their efforts had produced some interesting results. The Jensen brothers powered some of their cars with Ford V8s and, later, Lincoln V12s.

Sidney Allard made a strong case for the hybrid race car with a 160-horsepower Cadillac V8 Allard that captured third place at Le Mans in 1950. He didn't stop with that day, but his photograph appeared in several local newspapers, garnering publicity more for his attire than for his performance on the track. He quickly realized he had something of a marketing gimmick, and the overalls became his trademark.

Shelby's performance on the local circuit, especially with the Cad-Allards, came to the attention of John Wyer, team manager for Aston Martin, who asked Shelby to codrive an Aston Martin DB3 at Sebring, Florida. Wyer took on a mentor role during Shelby's relationship with Aston Martin.

Wyer provided intense training for the young driver and sent him to Europe in April 1954 to continue as a member of the Aston Martin team. At Aintree Shelby finished second against C-Type Jaguars, then rode along with Paul Frere at Le Mans. He also captured fifth place on his own at Monza.

When Shelby returned in August, he teamed with Donald Healey to help establish seventy land speed records in an Austin-Healey at the Bonneville Salt Flats in Utah. That same year he raced an Austin-Healey at the Carrera Panamericana in Mexico, a

grueling, pitiless, 2,178-mile (3,504.4km) monstrosity of a race that tested the soul of any driver. Just north of Oaxaca at the 175-kilometer (108½ miles) marker, Shelby smacked head-on into a huge boulder and flipped his Austin-Healey four times. He shattered his elbow and broke several other bones. Indians found him and nursed him with strong drinks before race medics could attend to his injuries.

Five months later, he was still recovering from the race. But he received an offer from Ferrari to drive with Phil Hill in a 3-liter

Monza Ferrari at Sebring. He accepted the invitation and had his arm supported by a special fiberglass cast, then taped the arm to the steering wheel. He performed well enough in that race to return in July 1955 to win the Torrey Pines race in a 4.1-liter Monza Ferrari, this time defeating Hill.

Carroll Shelby sits behind the wheel of a 4.9-liter Ferrari at the Palm Springs National Championship races in November 1956.

CARROLL SHELBY

Shelby's performance with Aston Martin and later with Ferraris and Maseratis earned him Driver of the Year honors from *Sports Illustrated* for two consecutive years, 1956 and 1957. His tenacity on the track also earned him an invitation to race in Europe, despite a serious crash during a practice run in September 1957 at Riverside Raceway, which required extensive plastic surgery to repair his face and fuse together three broken vertebrae.

Less than two years later he proved himself on the international circuit, taking first places in an Aston Martin DBR1/300 in the World's Manufacturers' Championship and at Le Mans.

Life literally and figuratively in the fast lane was catching up with Shelby. Hunting expeditions, too much Wild Turkey with his racing buddies, and a fierce competitiveness that sparked envy if not occasional fear in his track adversaries took their toll. As the 1960s dawned, he was sucking down nitroglycerin pills like candy to keep his bad heart ticking as he drove pell-mell on the track in Maseratis. He was a man who knew he was living on borrowed time.

A few weeks before the end of 1960, Shelby found himself at Riverside Raceway competing in the Times-Mirror Grand Prix for Sports Cars. With a nitroclycerin pill under his tongue, he struggled to make a respectable finish in his 3-liter Type 61 Birdcage Maserati. He got hammered, and finished fifth. It was his last race.

But the wily Texan wasn't about to sit still. The following year he opened a high-performance driving school by purchasing a ninety-dollar ad in *Sports Car Graphic*. With automotive designer Pete Brock preparing the curriculum, Shelby began teaching would-be race car drivers the ways of the track. But the school was really just an effort to pass the time. He had bigger fish to fry.

While he was driving his last race at Riverside, an idea began to solidify in Shelby's mind. He firmly believed that a production car could be built and sold relatively inexpensively, combining the best design and styling efforts of the European roadsters with beefy American power. He had no idea what form that roadster would take, nor did he have a clear picture of what kind of powerplant would move it. But in September 1961 he learned that AC Cars in England was not going to replenish its supply of Bristol engines for its two-seater roadster. Shelby wrote a letter to AC Cars owner Charles Hurlock proposing that Hurlock continue building his chassis to allow Shelby to develop a sports car to be powered by a V8 engine. Hurlock agreed and began shipping roadsters without engines and transmissions on February 2, 1962, to Shelby's shop in California. Meanwhile, Ford agreed to supply Shelby with 260-cubic-inch V8s.

The name of his new roadster came to him in a dream: "I woke up and jotted the name down on a pad, which I kept at my bedside—a sort of ideas pad—and went back to sleep. Next morning when I looked at the name 'Cobra,' I knew it was right." The very same day the 260 was installed on the AC chassis and was on the road by late afternoon. By March, Shelby-American began formal operations in Venice. A month later the CSX 2000 Cobra, painted pearlescent yellow, was shipped to the New York Auto Show and displayed with other Ford cars.

The development of Shelby-American and the number of orders flooding Shelby's Venice office after the New York Auto Show was more than the new operation could handle. Demand far exceeded supply, and Shelby found himself doing business on a shoestring budget. He had only one Cobra, and he had to make it available to several members of the automotive press. After each

test drive and story by an automotive journalist, Shelby had the car repainted so that it would appear he had several cars on hand to lend out to journalists. Even when he was down to his last twenty dollars, he spent it on lunch with an auto writer to hawk his new line of cars.

Shelby soon boosted the power of his Cobra from the 260 to a 289-cubic-inch engine that was an optional V8 for the new Ford Mustangs.

The Cobra's emergence on the track resulted in a battle of the titans between this new upstart roadster and the Corvette, which had stunning success on most American tracks but failed to achieve any greatness when pitted against Italian and British marques.

The Cobra's first race came at the Times Grand Prix in October 1962 with Bill Krause behind the wheel. In a preliminary run, Krause quickly demonstrated the Cobra's clear superiority over Corvette, but he broke a rear hub and was sidelined, leaving a 1963 Corvette Sting Ray to win the race. Even though the Cobra suffered through a series of mechanical failures in '63, the car was slowly becoming dependable as Shelby's team worked out the bugs and its drivers became more comfortable with it. In 1965, it won the International Manufacturers' Championship.

In the mid-1960s, the Cobra–Corvette duels were legendary, but the national SCCA race at Lake Garnett, Kansas, in July 1963 put to rest any doubts about which was the

superior car. Fielding a three-car team consisting of drivers Bob Johnson, Dave MacDonald (a former Vette driver), and Ken Miles, the Cobra faced off with the Corvette team of Dick Thompson, Don Yenko, and Grady Davis in what would prove to be a historic contest.

The 2.8-mile (4.5km) course around the 65-acre (26ha) Lake Garnett was a challenge, particularly through Muleshoe Corner, Snyder Corner, and the hairy corkscrew on the east side of the track. At the drop of the

terminated its long-term racing agreement. The AC Cobras went out of production as U.S. safety regulations tightened their squeeze on sports cars, which proved to be fatal to many small automakers.

Shelby pursued a number of other business interests in the '70s, including a safari operation in Africa and marketing his own brand of chili. In 1982, Chrysler chairman Lee Iacocca offered Shelby an opportunity to develop sports cars for the 1980s. Between 1986 and 1989 Shelby produced limited editions of high-performance Dodges, including the Charger GLH-S, the Shelby Lancer, the Shelby Dakota, and the turbocharged Shadow CSX-VNT.

But health problems were taking their toll. In 1991, Shelby's heart could barely keep up with him. He received a heart transplanted from a thirty-four-year-old Las Vegas gambler. In 1996, he received his second transplanted organ, this time a kidney donated by his son, Michael.

To raise money for the Shelby Heart Fund, Shelby dusted off a number of unused chassis originally earmarked for his '65 Cobras and began building new Cobras to 1965 specifications. He sells each unit at $500,000 a pop, with a portion of the sales earmarked for the fund. The venture has raised the eyebrows of the California Department of Vehicles and the ire of AC Cars—the latter claims the chassis belong to them. Nevertheless, production continues and the new Cobras are expected to be sold as 1965 models.

Shelby's Cobras shook the racing establishment to its core when it debuted in 1962. Although the Cobra was rough and unrefined compared to its European counterparts, Shelby succeeded like no other American carmaker—building competitive race cars to Italian, German, and British standards and winning on their own merit.

green flag, all three Cobras took comfortable leads in less than half a mile (804.5m) and performed surprisingly well at the corkscrew (Cobra chassis and suspension were designed in 1952, while Corvettes had state-of-the-art technology). The leads continued to increase until it was clear the Corvettes would not be able to make up any time. Johnson, MacDonald, and Miles finished first, second, and third respectively, while Thompson, Davis, and Yenko captured fourth, fifth, and sixth in that order. The race

left little doubt which American-made car was the leader on the track.

The Cobra also proved its mettle in international circles by defeating the formidable Ferrari and taking first place in the GT class and fourth overall at the 24-hour Le Mans in June 1964.

While Shelby was developing the prototype Cobra 427 and the 289 was dominating the SCCA A-production national races, Ford asked Shelby to build a special edition and racing version of the 1965 Mustang fastback.

He came up with the Mustang GT 350 with its distinctive white finish and blue racing stripes. He was also asked to supervise Ford's racing program for the factory's new GT-40, specifically designed to compete against Ferrari.

The GT 350 and the GT-40 were dominating on American circuits. And in June 1966, a trio of GT-40 Mark IIs finished 1-2-3 at Le Mans.

Ford continued its relationship with Shelby until February 1970, when the company

CHAPTER TWO

ALFA ROMEO

Born from the ashes of its bombed-out assembly plants in Milan and Naples during World War II, Alfa Romeo had lost none of its verve and tenacity when it jumped back into the road racing fray to establish a mass-produced sports car for the world.

The flames of war had barely been extinguished in Italy when Alfa Romeo brought out its 1.5-liter Type 158 Grand Prix cars. They set the racing circuit on its ear with their twin blowers that developed 350 horsepower from a 1479-cc 8-cylinder engine. When the Milan factory was up and running, it produced only a handful of 158s during those early months, but the 158's presence on the racing circuit was secure.

PREVIOUS PAGES: The forerunner to the top-performing postwar Alfa Romeos, this 1939 Corsa Spider engenders chic styling for Depression-era high society owners. By the dawn of the 1950s, Alfa Romeo was attempting to attract young family men as owners.

ABOVE: A rare 1937 Alfa Romeo 8C 2900 typifies the grace and elegance of Italian prewar design. Note the subtle splash of chrome along the bottom of the fenders, especially the fender skirts.

RIGHT: The luxurious interior of this 1933 Alfa Romeo 8C 2300 displays leather seats and an amazingly simple instrument cluster.

Anonima Lombarda Fabrica Automobili (ALFA) had gained fame for its exotic sports cars in the years between the wars and had an immense following among the upper middle class and the rich. After World War II, ALFA enhanced its reputation in the racing world and managed to mass-produce moderately priced sports without sacrificing quality.

The Italian company was originally founded as Società Anonima Italiana Darracq (SAID) for the Frenchman Alessandro Darracq, who attempted—and failed—to establish a market for taxis in Italy. His 1906 venture lasted only three years before it was taken over by ALFA. Engineer Nicola Romeo became owner of ALFA in 1911, then reorganized the company in 1918 to create Alfa Romeo.

Between 1924 and 1939, Alfa Romeo competed heavily and won its share of road races against the likes of Bentley, Mercedes-Benz, and Bugatti. A car by Alfa Romeo was perhaps the closest marque to the impeccable Bugatti as the best racing machine in Europe, and during a six-year period in the 1920s, the company captured eighteen international races. Engineer Vittorio Jano developed the supercharged 2.3- and 2.6-liter engines to make Alfa Romeo virtually unstoppable on the circuit.

The 1958 Alfa Romeo Sprint Veloce was a more sedate model for the Italian automaker's line, but it still displayed exceptional speed and nimble handling on the curves. The Veloce opened the door for potential upper middle class buyers, rather than only the upper crust of the luxury sports car market.

In 1925 it produced its 22/90 Alfa, the first so-called sports model for its two-seater design and long, tapered tail. The twin-cam 1752-cc engine model, dubbed the 1750 model, was introduced in 1929 and won the grueling 1,000-mile (1,609km) Italian Mille Miglia the following year. The Type B P3 2.9-liter model would follow and win seven Grand Prix races over a sixteen-month period before evolving into the 8C 2900 (2905-cc engine), which was equipped with twin superchargers and dual Weber carburetors to produce 180 horsepower.

Given Alfa Romeo's competitive edge following the war and its unwavering devotion to sporty two-seaters, it was something of a shock to Alfa enthusiasts to find that the company had determined that to turn its postwar devastation into a profitable company, it had to direct its products to the upper middle class.

The company unveiled the 6C 2500 at the 1947 Turin Salon. The new 6C 2500 evolved from the 1939–43 version and was powered by a 2443-cc twin-cam 6-cylinder engine. It came in the five-seat Turismo sedan, Sport, and Super Sport models.

Alfa's goal was not so much to produce a fine racing machine for the upper middle class driver, but to offer practical transportation with little emphasis on performance. While it remained a prestige car for the automaker, it was sluggish despite its 90 braking horsepower for the Sport model and 105 braking horsepower for the Super Sport. It was also somewhat overbodied by Alfa standards and mounted on an adequate chassis, but not the strongest available.

Very few 6C 2500s ever made it to the United States, and most Alfas produced before 1950 were used primarily for racing competition. Before production ceased in 1952, some 6C 2500s were shipped to the United States, but at a high price: $10,000 with a Pininfarina (also spelled Pinin Farina) body.

The 6C 2500 was hand-produced during those early years, and fewer than fifty were manufactured each month. But to stay alive, Alfa made some tough decisions—one of which was to enter the mass-production field. Alfa Romeo purists were distraught over what they perceived as the company's intent to abandon the high standards of performance and styling to produce a "people's car."

The Type 1900 made an impressive debut in 1950 with all-new postwar styling. The purists needn't have worried. The body of the Berlina—or sedan—was built in-house, while the coupe and cabriolet bodies were built by Ghia, Pininfarina, Bertone, Castagna, and Boano. All of the models had unibody construction. Despite the fact that the Alfa had never been intended to be a race car, drivers Piero Taruffi and Felice Bonetto finished fifth and ninth, respectively, in Mexico's punishing, rough-and-tumble Carrera Panamericana, in 1950. Taruffi averaged 76.5 mph (123kph) while Bonetto hit 77.8 mph (125.1kph). Top speed for the 1900 Sprint cabriolet hit about 100 mph (160.9kph), while the Sprint coupe could achieve 106 mph (170.5kph). All of this was made possible with a twin-overhead-cam 4-cylinder engine with a 1884-cc displacement. It had a 7.5:1 compression ratio for 80 braking horsepower at 4800 rpm.

As far as the U.S. market was concerned, Alfa Romeo came into its own with the Giulietta, a model that was smaller than the 1900 but nimble in heavy traffic and targeted toward the young family man. It came as a four-door sedan, coupe, and roadster, and far exceeded the dreams of Alfa Romeo brass with nearly 200,000 produced between 1954 and 1965.

The Sprint coupe was produced in 1954 and was basically a two-seater, although it featured a very small rear seat. The Sprint's body was built by coachbuilder Nuccio Bertone Carrozzeria and was manufactured until 1962. It sold for about $4,200 in the United States with production totaling about twenty-two thousand.

The Giulietta got off to a rocky start. Alfa Romeo had planned to expand its facilities and increase its production. A lottery was held to sell cars to ticket holders, but design and development were delayed. The production of the Giulietta was nearly tainted by scandal, with allegations surfacing that Alfa Romeo was committing fraud by offering cars that did not exist. Eventually, Bertone began building the 2-plus-2 Sprint coupe, and the Giulietta was introduced at the Turin auto show. Initially, only enough cars were made to supply the lottery winners, but by the end of the production year in 1954, the initial run totaled 3,826 units.

Whatever headaches Alfa Romeo endured to get the Giulietta off the ground were soon forgotten. Here was a lively sports car that satisfied not only the younger driver needing a roadster fix, but also the older driver looking for a little spring in the step of his car, giving him the youthful sports car feel. The Giulietta sat on a 93.5-inch (237.4cm) wheelbase (the Giulietta Spider on an 86.6-inch [219.9cm] wheelbase) with an overall length of 153 inches (388.6cm) and a curb weight of 2,088 pounds (947.9kg). Under the hood was a 1290-cc inline, dual-overhead-cam 4-cylinder engine with an 8:1 compression ratio for 65 braking horsepower at 6000 rpm.

Almost delicate, if not feminine, in appearance, the Giulietta Sprint sat only 5 inches (12.7cm) above the ground. It demanded precision driving. It was not a sports car for the ham-fisted driver. Its road handling—with a solid rear axle, front independent suspension, coil springs, and four large, aluminum-finned drum brakes—made it a nimble little fella on hilly and curvy terrain. It usually managed 0–60 mph (0–96.5kph) in about 13 seconds, depending on the Sprint's age and whether it had a passenger along for the ride. Top speed averaged between 99 and 103 mph (159.2 and 165.7kph).

Road & Track magazine noted that the Giulietta was a "modern Juliet . . . a wench to win the heart of any motor-minded Romeo before he even gets out of second gear."

The Giulia Spider was introduced in late 1962 for the 1963 model year to replace the venerable Giulietta, and had an engine displacement enlarged from 1290 to 1570 cc. Then came the Alfa Duetto 1600 Spider, which was nothing like the Giulietta. The bullet-shaped design by coachbuilder Pininfarina was an interpretation of aerodynamic styling that was revolutionary even for the Italians.

The Duetto made its first appearance at the 1966 Geneva show. Its sleek design was inspired by the 1959 Disco Volante, and that basic design would endure through the 1980s, long after the Duetto name was dropped by Alfa Romeo.

Initial reaction to the car's styling was mixed, with the memory of the Giulietta and Giulia still fresh in enthusiasts' minds. It maintained the trademark Alfa Romeo grille, but everything else was different. Headlamps were now recessed deep into the fenders and the side panels were deeply channeled and scalloped.

The engine had a boosted compression ratio of 9.1:1 to generate 125 braking horsepower at 6000 rpm, compared to the Giulia Sprint GT, which provided 109 braking horsepower. The new engine allowed drivers to hit 60 mph (96.5kph) in 11.3 seconds. The Duetto sat a bit higher than the Giulietta, at 5.8 inches (14.7cm) from the ground on an 88.6-inch (225cm) wheelbase, and had a curb weight of 2,195 pounds (996.5kg).

Instrumentation on board the Duetto was fairly impressive: an 8000-rpm tachometer; a 140-mph (225.2kph) speedometer; a trip odometer; fuel, oil pressure, and water temperature gauges; and warning lights for the generator and fuel level.

Certainly, there were misgivings about the overall design and execution of the Duetto Spider, but driving it was another matter. *Road & Track* reported in its September 1966 issue: "The overall impression is one of great responsiveness, and the feeling that the car is an extension of the driver at the controls is unmistakably clear. The steering is excellent—light, accurate, and among the best we've ever encountered in any car."

By the end of the 1960s, the Duetto name was abandoned in favor of simply calling the open-topped car the Spider. Now the 1750, it sported a new 1779-cc engine to produce 132 horsepower. The engine was bored out for the 1972 model year to give the four-banger a 1962-cc displacement to produce 129 horsepower. It was then named the 2000.

The V8 2593-cc Montreal was introduced in 1972 as the new 2000 after it was first given a public viewing at the Expo '67 in Montreal. The Montreal was Alfa Romeo's effort at attracting the luxury market with Bertone-inspired coupe styling and mid-engine design. Sitting on a 92.5-inch (234.9cm) wheelbase, it could achieve 60 mph (96.5kph) in 8 seconds with a top speed of 132 mph (212.3kph). Never certified for sale in the United States, its production was relatively low. Only 668 were manufactured in 1971, 2,377 in '72, 302 in '73, 205 in '74, 323 in '75, and only a handful—23 units—in 1976.

The 2000 Spider Veloce remained virtually unchanged through the 1980s, drawing criticism for what some sports car enthusiasts deemed an aging design. Yet the consistent styling over twenty years allowed it to remain timeless and therefore attractive to the collector market.

The basic Spider design remained until 1991, when a restyled version was put on the market with the same engine but was made available with either manual or automatic transmission.

Credit must be given to Alfa Romeo for its presence in the U.S. market, a rare feat for an Italian automaker. Its basic styling foundation, reliability, quick handling, and relatively moderate prices have kept it a viable offering for U.S. buyers.

Alfa Romeo 2000 Spider (1964)

SPECIFICATIONS

Weight — 2,200 pounds (999.8kg)

Tire size — 165HR14

Engine type — Inline, dual-overhead cam, four-cylinder

Bore and stroke — 3.31 X 3.48

Displacement — 1962 cc

Compression ratio — 9.0:1

Carburetor — Spica mechanical fuel injection

Braking horsepower — 129 @ 5800 rpm

Torque — 130 lbs.-ft. @ 3700 rpm

Transmission — five-speed manual

DIMENSIONS

Wheelbase — 88.6 in. (225.0cm)

Length — 166.2 in. (422.1cm)

Height — 48.8. in. (123.9cm)

Width — 64.1 in. (162.8cm)

Front tread — 52.1 in. (132.3cm)

Rear tread — 50.1 in. (127.2cm)

PERFORMANCE

0–60 mph (0–96.5 kph) — N/A

Top speed — N/A

CHAPTER THREE

ASTON MARTIN

I t seemed as if British automakers were in a perpetual struggle to maintain a competitive edge against Italian and German factory race teams. Inferior-quality machines and a tendency to have even their best vehicles saddled with underwhelming powerplants often made English drivers no more than spectators in some of Europe's most prestigious endurance races.

For a brief, shining period in the 1950s and early 1960s, Aston Martin came closest of any British carmaker to providing winning teams for the Union Jack.

ownership over the decades, but the quality of its motorcars never suffered from the lack of stability. In 1930, Aston Martin debuted the stunning four-seater International, which could reach speeds of up to 80 mph (128.7kph). Although not truly a speedster, its superb handling and excellent braking system won kudos from its drivers.

In 1932, R. Gordon Sutherland, who was devoted to racing and the advanced designs of sports cars, was the next owner to come along and tinker with a winning product. He redesigned the transmission and eliminated the heavy torque tube by introducing the Mark II sports model and, a short while later, the Ulster, which broke the 1.5-liter engine record at Le Mans in 1935.

Before World War II broke out, Sutherland introduced the prototype Atom with its streamlined body, Cotal Electric gearbox, coil springs, and independent suspension. The Atom never saw production, as England geared up for the war effort, but it did serve as a foundation for Aston Martin's entry into the postwar sports car market.

After the war, Aston Martin was caught in limbo for nearly two years while it sought funding. Sutherland found his company's savior in David Brown, chairman of the David Brown Corporation, a tractor- and gear-manufacturing firm. Sutherland and Aston Martin engineer Claude Hill remained on the company board after Brown's arrival.

Crucial to Aston Martin's survival was the acquisition by Brown of Lagonda, a small motorcar-manufacturing company with a design contract with W.O. Bentley. Brown wanted Lagonda's engines to be installed in the Aston Martins. To that end, he formed Aston Martin Lagonda Ltd. in 1947. Brown was interested in Lagonda's 2.6-liter 6-cylinder twin-overhead-cam engine, designed by Bentley.

Robert Bamford and Lionel Martin, dealers of the Singer automobile, wanted a sophisticated racing car that was equal to Bugatti in every way. They found a Bugatti-designed 1908 Isotta-Fraschini chassis and installed a 1.4-liter Coventry-Simplex L-head 4-cylinder engine. They named it Aston for the Aston Clinton hill climb that used to be run by Singer. Martin allowed his name to be placed on the machine, making the formal name Aston Martin.

Aston Martin immediately made a good name for itself in early racing circles. Its Coventry-Simplex engine helped Aston Martin break ten world racing records during the 1930s.

By 1924, the Charnwood family took over the company, but it soon collapsed under several financial problems and was then purchased by "Bert" Bertelli and W.S. Renwick. The company would experience a series of changes in

Under owner David Brown's tutelage, the Aston Martin DB Series would win numerous races. The DB3S captured eight racing victories in 1953 alone. And the DB4 was soon counted on as a serious rival to Maserati and Ferrari. Equipped with a lightweight Zagato body, David Brown's GT versions, placed on a short wheelbase, generated 325 horsepower to make Aston Martin one of the top contenders on the racing circuit.

Bugatti had already been a name synonymous with quality motoring when Aston Martin came onto the racing scene in 1913.

The first postwar Aston Martin off the assembly line was the DB1 ("DB" for David Brown's initials). It was based on the Atom design by Claude Hill, but only fifteen DB1s were built. It was placed on a 108-inch (274.3cm) wheelbase and developed a braking horsepower of 90 at 4750 rpm. It could hit about 95 mph (152.8kph) if pampered right.

The DB2 was a much more successful effort and the first real Aston Martin produced under Brown's supervision. The fastback coupe and drophead coupe posted better production numbers than the DB1 with 309 and 97 units, respectively. Maintaining a basic body style through the end of the 1950s, it embodied all the characteristics of past and future Aston Martins. The 2580-cc 6-cylinder engine developed 107 horsepower at 5000 rpm, with 60 mph (96.5kph) achieved at 12.4 seconds. The DB2 came with an optional

Vantage 6-cylinder engine with the same displacement as the standard six, but with a boosted compression ratio from 6.5:1 to 8.16:1 for 125 horsepower.

The DB2 was in production from May 1950 until April 1953. The DB2-4 was also available as a two-seater with an "occasional"—read very small—seat in the rear. The DB Mark III Series superseded the DB2-4 and featured disc brakes, giving Aston Martin the distinction of being the first production car to be equipped with them.

Helping sales during the 1950s was Aston Martin's performance on the racetrack. The DBR1/300 model took top honors in the World Sports Car Championship in 1959. With 3-liter engines, Aston Martin captured six first places in World Championship races, setting five lap records, and also won first place at the 1959 Le Mans and World's Manufacturers' Championship.

The DB4 debuted in the fall of 1958, employing an all-new body design, a more rigid chassis, and a larger 6-cylinder engine. Placed on a pressed-steel platform frame and with an inch (2.5cm) sliced off the wheelbase—cutting it down to 98 inches (248.9cm), the DB4, while considered a four-seater, was

probably more accurately a 2-plus-2 fastback. It now offered a 2922-cc engine displacement for 162 horsepower at 5500 rpm.

In the early 1960s, Aston Martin demonstrated its prowess on the racetrack and in marketing through its DB4GT and DB4 Zagato racing models and the famous 1964 Aston Martin DB5, recognizable worldwide as the James Bond car.

The DB4GT was really a semiracing vehicle with only seventy-five units produced. It was smaller and lighter and had a more rounded front than the street models. It rode on a wheelbase 5 inches (12.7cm) smaller—93 inches (236.2cm)—than the standard DB4 and had cowled headlamps recessed into the front fenders. Its panels were constructed of 18-gauge magnesium alloy, and it weighed 2,706 pounds (1,228.5kg). Under its bonnet was a howling 3670-cc 6-cylinder engine with a 9:1 compression ratio to develop a masculine 302 braking horsepower, compared to just the 263 ponies powering the standard DB4. The engine also came equipped with a standard dual ignition, twin distributors, and a pair of spark plugs for each cylinder. Top speed for this monster sports car was 142 mph (228.4kph) with 0–60 mph (0–96.5kph) in almost the blink of an eye—6.4 seconds. Introduced at the 1959 Paris Auto Show as the David Brown Aston Martin DB4GT, it was promoted by the company as "embodying the lessons of ten years of endeavor on the most arduous race circuits of the world."

Lighter by 106 pounds (48.1kg) than the DB4GT was the Zagato, a fastback coupe. Bumpers were optional. It performed better than the GT model in the 0–60 mph (0–96.5kph) contest with a 6.1-second time and a top speed of 153 mph (246.1kph).

But the most famous of all Aston Martins was the legendary James Bond car. Introduced in late 1963, the DB5 was featured in the movies *Goldfinger* and *Thunderball* as the ultimate dream car for spies. An enlarged bore gave it a 3995-cc displacement with 282 horsepower, while the optional Vantage engine offered 325 horsepower. More intriguing—but hardly practical or necessary for the common driver—were the incorporated machine guns, passenger ejector seat, hydraulic overrider rams, and equipment to eject oil, nails, and smoke to ward off villains bent on world domination.

> The Aston Martin that made the marque world-famous: the 1965 DB5 James Bond car. Introduced in 1963, it was powered by a 3995-cc engine to generate 282 horsepower. It was featured in such movies as *Goldfinger* and *Thunderball*. Note the license plate, "007 JB."

The Aston Martin Lagonda would ride on the coattails of the Bond films, but Brown decided to cease competitive racing in order to concentrate on redefining Aston Martin's range. However, Aston Martin finished the season in late 1963 with a stunning win at Monza by Roy Salvadori in a GT Aston Martin. Despite the prestige, times were tough for the carmaker. Changing tastes in motoring and the financial instability of the Italy-based Touring coachbuilders hit the automaker hard. Demand for costly cars in England, in particular, dropped significantly in the late 1960s. And automotive writers began to complain about the DB6's engine noises, less-than-desirable handling on rough roads, and difficult steering.

By the early 1970s, it appeared that David Brown was ready to give up his beloved company after twenty-five years, when it became apparent that Aston Martin was not going to fit in his long-range plans. He sold the company on February 16, 1972, to Company Developments Ltd., a Birmingham-based group of businessmen. Brown maintained a seat on the board of directors. William Willson became president and chairman of the board.

The "DB" designation was dropped from the 1972 models and the cars were now simply the Aston Martin V8 and the Aston Martin Vantage.

Engine displacement continued to grow, with the V8 now at 5340 cc to provide 350 horsepower. Wheelbase had also grown, to 102.75 inches (260.9cm), and automatic transmission was a major option. But company fortunes were in peril, and Company Developments opted to sell Aston Martin Lagonda in 1974. For a six-month period in

1974–75, production was stopped as the company sought funding and new managers.

In June 1975, Americans George Mindeli and Peter Sprague and Englishman Alan Curtis purchased the floundering company, and quickly introduced the new Aston Martin Lagonda; the Lagonda moniker hadn't been used since the demise of the Lagonda Rapide more than two decades earlier. The new body design by William Towns was striking in its appearance, a thoroughly modern effort that rivaled virtually every contemporary sports car on the market. However, by today's standards, it may have lost a bit of its luster, as many 1970s and early 1980s sports cars adopted similar designs.

Still, the Aston Martin remained a sports car to be reckoned with. In 1977, the V8 Vantage engine saw its displacement jump to 5340 cc to give it more than 350 horses and a 15 percent boost in power. Initial ratings for the Vantage were as high as 400 horsepower. The convertible Volante was an even meaner-looking machine with its deep front air dam and large Cibie driving lamps in front of a blanked grille. It also featured a rear air spoiler.

In the early 1980s, Aston Martin Lagonda was sold, this time to Victor Gauntlett, owner of Pace Petroleum, a private petroleum distribution company, and C.H. Industrials, a public company chaired by Tim Hearley.

Aston Martin returned to the racing circuit in 1982 with drivers Robin Hamilton, who operated an Aston Martin distributorship in Staffordshire, and Victor Gauntlett in asso-

Aston Martin DB4 Series (1959)

SPECIFICATIONS

Weight — 2,884 pounds (1,309.3kg)

Tire size — 6.00 × 16

Engine type — Inline, dual overhead-cam 6-cylinder

Bore and stroke — 3.62 × 3.6 in.

Displacement — 3670 cc

Compression ratio — 8.25:1

Carburetor — Two SU carburetors

Braking horsepower — 240 @ 5500 rpm

Torque — 240 lbs.-ft. @ 4250 rpm

Transmission — 4-speed manual

DIMENSIONS

Wheelbase — 98 in. (248.9cm)

Length — 176.4 in. (448.0cm)

Height — 51.5 in. (130.8cm)

Width — 66 in. (167.6cm)

Front tread — 54 in. (137.1cm)

Rear tread — 53.5 in. (135.8cm)

PERFORMANCE

0–60 mph (0–96.5 kph) — 8.5 seconds

Quarter mile (402.3m) — 16.8 seconds

Top speed — 141 mph (226.8 kph)

ciation with Nimrod Racing Automobiles. The partnership was formed to race in the World Endurance Championship class. During their first year on the track, Aston Martin's performance was less than stellar. They finished third at the Championship and seventh at Le Mans.

Just a year later, Automotive Investments, distributors of Aston Martin, purchased the Pace Petroleum shares of the company. In 1987, Ford Motor Co. purchased 75 percent of the company's shares.

During the same year, the Zagato, with a 5340-cc V8 engine and capable of hitting 60 mph (96.5kph) in just 4.7 seconds, rolled off the assembly plant in Italy. Only fifty of them were produced.

The Virage was introduced at the October 1988 Birmingham International Motor Show to replace the Vantage V8. It featured a hand-formed wedge-shaped aluminum body with minimal chrome and flush rectangular headlamps. It was an extremely clean-looking car unlike anything on the road and a vast improvement over the 1980s offerings. It kept the same 5340-cc V8 engine, but the compression ratio was boosted to 9.5:1 for a braking horsepower of 330 at 6000 rpm.

The Virage was sold in England in 1989 but didn't reach the United States until the summer of 1990. Production totals were not released by the company, but exports to the United States were very few.

In September 1991, Gauntlett, who had served as executive chairman of Aston Martin Lagonda through its many changes in ownership during the 1980s, resigned to make way for new chairman Walter Hayes, the former vice-chairman of Ford of Europe.

In 1995, the company produced a one-off, or "Solitaire" edition, of the Virage Volante. The one-of-a-kind car was sold with a set of Cartier jewelry for $1.25 million. The unidentified buyer disappeared with it, and the whereabouts of the car, the jewelry, and the buyer today are unknown.

ABOVE: A 1987 Aston Martin Vantage Zagato with a 5340-cc V8 engine that could achieve 0–60 mph (0–96.5kph) in 4.7 seconds. Only fifty of the 5340-cc models were produced.

CHAPTER FOUR

AUSTIN-HEALEY

Austin-Healey was the product of two disparate companies that served two very distinct motoring markets. The famed 100 roadster was developed not as a result of the daring partnership of two men with the same vision, but as the result of a contest to produce a new sports car using Austin components.

Austin was known for producing quality saloons and taxis. This was the company that created the wildly popular Mini-Coopers and Austin Americas that attracted attention in the United States for their small size and panache, which made them suitable economical answers to the Volkswagen.

and was developing vehicles that would compete and win in 1,000-mile (1,609km) races. The company later developed the Austin Seven, a very small four-seater. An estimated 100,000 Sevens were sold by 1929.

Variations of the Seven were produced through the 1930s and into World War II, as many were manufactured for the military. Many Austins returned to civilian use after the war. The first postwar Austins were the A40 Devon and Dorset, which featured built-in headlamps and rear-opening doors, and were notable for the absence of running boards.

The Austin hit the U.S. market in the 1960 model year with its popular Mini. It featured a modest 848-cc engine that generated 37 horsepower at 5500 rpm, 1 horsepower more than the Volkswagen at the time. The Mini and the high-performance Mini-Cooper debuted in 1962. Sales of the Minis were exceptional. In 1963, for example, 250,000 Minis were sold.

Automaker Donald Healey was not really competing with the Austin. Rather, he loved the idea of a true roadster and focused his attention on two-seaters, although his coupes also proved popular. A talented European race driver in the 1920s and 1930s, Healey became associated with the

PREVIOUS PAGES: The 1956 Austin-Healey 100 is one of the most popular British marques, sought after by enthusiasts looking for the most attractive 1950s sports car. With its clamshell grille, wire wheels, and simple design, the Austin-Healey epitomizes 1950s speed and styling.

ABOVE: The Austin Seven, like this 1928 model, is a very small four-seater that gained wide popularity during the 1920s. By the end of the decade an estimated 100,000 units were sold.

RIGHT: The Healey Silverstone, named for the famed British race course, was the first true sports car produced by Donald Healey. The prewar look of this 1950 model features motorcycle fenders and low-cut doors. Headlamps are hidden behind the grille. On the sides of the bonnet are Buick-like portholes.

Healey, during its short run in early postwar England, built fixed-head coupes but also produced some very fine sports cars, including the Healey Silverstone roadster.

Austin can trace its automotive roots to 1906 with its 5-liter 25/30 model. Herbert Austin had founded the company

British Motor Corporation (BMC) and also worked as technical director for Triumph.

Healey founded his own automaking company but used assembled parts from other builders to keep production costs low. He soon became associated with the American automaker Nash, developing some fine roadsters to help Nash create a new market aside from its passenger cars and give it some prestige with American buyers.

The Nash-Healey debuted at the 1950 auto shows in London and Paris. It featured an aluminum body on a Healey chassis with a modified Nash Ambassador 3847-cc engine to develop 125 horsepower at 4000 rpm. Nash-Healeys were assembled by Healey at the Warwick plant and sold by Nash dealers in the United States. A coupe was added to the Nash-Healey line and the relationship with the American company remained intact until August 1954.

Donald Healey produced sports cars on his own in the late 1940s and early 1950s. His first effort was a prototype sports tourer. It was powered by a 2.4-liter engine and later a 3-liter six. Its body featured pontoon-style fenders, a split windshield, leather upholstery, polished walnut interior woodwork, and even a radio as standard equipment.

The Silverstone was Healey's first true sports car, and was produced from 1949 to 1951. Named after the Grand Prix race course in England, the Silverstone had a decidedly prewar look to it, with motorcycle-style fenders, low-cut doors, and a basic rectangular windshield. It also adopted an American characteristic: Buick-style portholes behind the front fenders. Only 105 were built to complement the other 676 Healey models produced during that period.

It seemed like a natural for Austin and Healey to join forces, and as mentioned before, it was due to a contest sponsored by BMC, producers of Austin. The contest was for the best sports car design, with the winner to have the car realized using Austin components.

Healey's 100 won the contest and was honored at the 1952 Earl's Court motor show in London. When production began at Austin's Longbridge, Birmingham, plant, the car was renamed the Austin-Healey 100.

Despite a modest output of only 90 braking horsepower at 4000 rpm from a 2660-cc Austin A90 engine, the 100 was a light roadster a tad heavier than 2,000 pounds (908kg) and placed on a relatively short wheelbase of 90 inches (228.6cm). Its cornering was responsive and it could hit top speeds of more than 103 mph (165.7kg). The body featured long, flowing lines, a rather long bonnet, and an egg-shaped grille that would remain on Austin-Healey roadsters through the 1956 model year. Bucket seats for the driver and passenger were designed to hold riders in their seats through hard cornering. An astounding 10,688 100s were produced during 1953 and 1954.

Ever conscious that it was performance and racing records that sold cars, Donald Healey took a modified 100 to the Bonneville Salt Flats in Utah and hit 142.6 mph (229.5kph) over 1 mile (1.6km). Another modified 100 managed to reach 122 mph (196.3kph) in a 2,000-mile (3,218km) endurance test.

The 1955 models differed little from the initial run of 100s. The same 2660-cc engine was featured, but a 100M model generated 110 horsepower. There were only fifty units produced (some sources say fifty-five) of a special model, the 100S, but it bears discussion.

The 100S—S for Sebring—was a lightweight, stripped-down, aluminum-bodied car, featuring a highly modified 2660-cc engine that provided 132 horsepower at 4700 rpm. It was conceived by Donald Healey primarily as a marketing and development tool. In 1954, famed race driver Stirling Moss sailed to a third-place finish at the Sebring

The 1958 Austin-Healey Sprite was a favorite among American buyers. The bugeye Sprite sat on an 80-inch (203.2cm) wheelbase and was powered by an adequate 948-cc engine to generate 43 horsepower. It was considered very nimble on the roadway. The front clip opens as a single unit.

12-hour race. All 100S models were built at the Healey Warwick plant instead of the Austin Birmingham facility. Healey had forty-seven units painted in American racing colors of white and blue, and converted one 100S to a coupe for his own personal use. Twenty-five 100S models were shipped to the United States.

Among the unique features of the 100S are the right-hand drive only, an aluminum head, no overdrive, four-wheel Dunlop disc brakes, a Healey wood-rim steering wheel, a 25-gallon (94.6L) fuel tank with quick-release filler cap, twin fuel pumps, a remote oil cooler, solid rivet body construction, seat belts, and Lucas Le Mans headlamps.

The sports car maker stumbled in the 1957 model year with the 100-6, a four-seater on a slightly longer wheelbase of 92 inches (233.6cm), which was powered by a 2632-cc 6-cylinder engine. It was heavier than previous models by more than 400 pounds (181.6kg), but cranked only 102 horsepower at 4600 rpm, making performance less than desirable. It felt sluggish in cornering, although its speed wasn't as bad as its reputation over the years would suggest. It could hit 60 mph (96.5kph) in 12.9 seconds with a top speed of about 104 mph (167.3kph).

Still, the 100-6 met with considerable criticism during its early years from owners who complained bitterly that it was underpowered and had less than effective drum brakes. Early mechanical problems included a head with an integral two-port inlet manifold, which made it difficult to get a good charge into cylinders.

Donald Healey felt a need to install rear seats to accommodate families, but the seats were so tiny that they were comfortable only for small children. The most noticeable difference in appearance was a redesigned oval grille, which did away with the old shell-shaped one. A new hood scoop also was added, but the smooth, flowing lines remained true to the first 100s.

The 100-6 models were replaced by the 3000 versions in 1959. These big Healeys enjoyed a 2912-cc engine displacement and disc brakes, both a direct answer to critics' beefs about the performance of the 100-6 models.

Like the 1958 four-seater Ford Thunderbird—which initially drew heavy fire from purists who loved their two-seaters—the 100-6 in recent years has gained respect from enthusiasts who are now beginning to realize that performance isn't as bad as first thought and perhaps a four-seater was a good idea. And despite lukewarm press reviews, 10,826 four-seaters were produced among the total of 57,325 Austin-Healeys during 1957–58.

Austin-Healey made its biggest splash in 1958 with its bugeye Sprite, a tiny (80-inch [203.2cm] wheelbase), moder-

ately powered roadster that complemented the bigger sports cars. The bugeye (or frogeye in England) was named for its protruding headlamps mounted on the bonnet. It performed exceptionally well on the road, especially on curves, with its tight rack and pinion steering. Its little 948-cc engine generated just 43 horsepower, but that was sufficient for its size and what it was expected to do on the road. A unique feature was access to the engine, with the entire front end hinged at the front to lift it upward. There was no boot space to speak of, but storage access was available behind the leather-upholstered seats.

The bugeye Sprite was the brainchild of Leonard Lord, who was associated with BMC. By the mid-1950s, the sports car market began to display signs that bigger, faster cars were becoming more expensive to purchase and maintain. The market for these big monsters was shrinking. Lord envisioned a compact, economical, yet exciting sports car. Lord had a reputation as a hard-nosed executive who was always conscious of England's position in the motoring industry. He gave Healey permission to manufacture the Sprite, which made its debut in May 1958. Donald Healey's son, Geoffrey, was in on the design.

Two months after its introduction, race drivers Willy Cave and John Sprinzel led a team of Sprites to winning their class at the Alpine rally. Also in July 1958, John Anstice-Brown drove a Sprite to victory in the Leinster Trophy handicap race in Ireland.

Power increased steadily over the years, and by the mid-sixties, the Sprite generated 59 horsepower.

Production for the Sprite's first year was 8,279, with many cars being shipped to the United States. Production would climb dramatically over the next two years, with 21,566 in '59 and 18,665 in '60.

The second-generation Sprite Mk II debuted in 1961 with a squared front and rectangular grille, eliminating the endearing bugeye appearance. It was a conventionally designed sports car in every way, with a standard bonnet and boot. 41gained respectability, but lost a lot of its personality in the process.

The Sprite carried on through 1970, after which it continued for a year as simply an Austin, then was discontinued. Its near-identical cousin, the MG Midget, continued through 1977.

In 1949, the A90 Austin Atlantic broke sixty-three stock car racing records at Indianapolis, serving as a harbinger of what was to come with the Austin-Healey. These two Austin Atlantics are 1950 models.

STIRLING MOSS

He retired from auto racing at the age of thirty-two after cracking up his Lotus at Goodwood in 1962. He was a perennial second-place finisher for the World Championship and, at one point in his career, had a reputation for breaking up his cars. He played the romantic nomad on the racing circuit, inspiring the likes of such actors as Steve McQueen and James Garner in race films. And he knew how to play the crowd with the wave of a hand, knowing full well that a popular driver brought lucrative offers from car sponsors.

Stirling Moss was Great Britain's media darling of the 1950s and 1960s, and the attention was well deserved. After World War II, England always came up a day late and a dollar short behind Germany and Italy in road racing. It hurt the proud Brits to see their former adversaries at war burning up the track and leaving their drivers in the wake of blue smoke and oil.

So when Moss emerged as a serious driver in 1951, he soon charmed the public with his solid racing skills in typical straight-arm fashion against the steering wheel. It's too bad that he was often saddled with inferior British racing cars, and sadder still—at least for England—that he often turned to Mercedes-Benz, Maserati, and Ferrari to achieve some of his greatest racing successes. But he never raced a foreign car without it being painted British green or carrying the Union Jack.

During his ten-year career, he participated in five hundred motoring events, finishing in 376 and placing first 217 times. He covered 3,362 laps and 12,508 miles (20,175km) but never won the coveted World Drivers Championship.

Born on September 17, 1929, Stirling Moss was the son of famed race driver Alfred Moss. The elder Moss had been a premier driver in the 1920s and 1930s. When Stirling was seventeen years old, his father encouraged him to drive the little 500-cc rear-engine Cooper in Formula Three racing events in England. By the time he was twenty-one, Stirling had won his first Gold Star Award, given by the British Racing Drivers' Club. He went on to win a total of ten such awards, more than any other driver.

Once Moss' dominance on the track became apparent, Enzo Ferrari attempted to lure him to his factory team with promises of making him a champion. Moss refused the offer, first probably due to his dislike for Ferrari (more than a few drivers complained about working for Ferrari), and second due to his intense nationalistic pride. Setting aside his professional judgment for the love of his country, Moss turned to British makes to further his career. His relationship with such makes as HWM, Connaught, and BRM were not successful.

The Connaught, for example, made a brief run at a series of racing events in the late 1940s and early 1950s before petering out by 1957. The Connaught was powered by a 1767-cc 4-cylinder engine that was capable of putting out 410 horsepower. Created by race driver and Bugatti owner Rodney Clarke and placed on a 90-inch (228.6cm) wheelbase, the Connaught debuted at Silverstone in June 1949. But it never achieved the dreams established by Clarke, and even Moss couldn't make it a winner.

Stirling Moss waves a victory salute after capturing first place in the 1955 Mille Miglia at Brescia, Italy, in May 1955. Moss was only twenty-four years old when he won the punishing race, averaging 98.5 mph (158.4 kph) over 990 miles (1,592.9km) and shattering the previous record of 88.0 mph (141.5 kph).

Moss was keenly aware of the limitations of British cars, at least when put up against Ferrari and Maserati. In 1954, he turned to the Maserati 250F to begin a serious climb to the top of the racing ladder. Moss also recognized that to be successful in a business as glamorous as auto racing, he would have to develop a persona that matched the romance of his profession. While he was a student of the art of racing, he liked having fun and saw himself much like a performer on a stage.

In an era where cars didn't move as quickly as they do today, Moss had the habit of waving to the crowd at virtually every opportunity. He'd blow kisses to pretty girls, salute a mechanic he knew, and wave to the

Stirling Moss hugs the corner in his Mercedes-Benz on his way to victory in the grueling Mille Miglia near Rome. Juan Manuel Fangio, also driving a Mercedes, took second place.

crowds in the grandstand. He was truly a charismatic man who loved the attention and adored the fame that went with racing. But he also saw the opportunity to impress race organizers and potential sponsors, who were willing to pay a lot of cash to drivers who brought in the crowds.

Not everyone cared for Moss as a man. The legendary Phil Hill once described him as "as much a nut case as the rest of us," but respected his ability behind the wheel and his relationship with racing fans.

His tastes in cars other than British ones, like the Maserati, whetted his appetite for other marques. In 1955, he was invited to drive for Mercedes-Benz. It led to what may have been his finest performance as a race driver when he won the Italian Mille Miglia in a 300 SLR roadster. He became the only Englishman ever to win the Mille Miglia—considered perhaps the most difficult road race in the world—and only the second non-Italian. Moss and his navigator, Denis Jenkinson, drove the 1,000 miles (1,609km) in

a little more than 10 hours. Their top speed was 176 mph (283.1kph) with a course average of 98.5 mph (158.4kph). Mercedes would later abandon road racing after Pierre Levegh crashed his 300 SLR into the grandstand at the 1955 Le Mans, killing himself and almost ninety other people.

Moss also did well at Aintree in England that year, with a win in a Mercedes-Benz W196 powered by a 2.5-liter straight-eight engine. The W196 was the brainchild of Rudolf Uhlenhaut's Mercedes Racing Department and was engineered by Dr. Fritz Nallinger. With a braking horsepower of 310 at 8000 rpm, Moss could hit a top speed of 187 mph (300.8kph). His fastest lap on the 434.5-kilometer circuit was a sliver over 2 minutes with a top speed of 89 mph (144.4kph).

The Mercedes W196 would be one of Moss' most enjoyable cars on the track. While he considered the Maserati 250F his sentimental favorite, the Mercedes remained his more practical choice, a car that he had absolute confidence in to win races.

Moss told Nigel Roebuck in *Grand Prix Greats*, "I knew that if I didn't go off the road, I was either going to win or finish second to [driver Juan Manuel] Fangio. It was much more reliable than the Maserati, but the 250F was a lot more fun because you could overdrive it."

In 1955, Moss participated in six Grand Prix races, winning one and coming in second in the World Drivers Championship. In fact, he would finish the World Drivers Championship in second place four times and third place three times between 1955 and 1961.

These were wins with excellent machines. But he also suffered through some tough luck, having a crankshaft bust on an Aston Martin or a rear wheel break on a Lotus. Many times he climbed into a car that was lightened to compensate for power shortcomings. It was a dangerous business, putting his life on the line with a car like that.

In Charles Fox's *Great Racing Cars and Drivers*, Phil Hill wrote, "There was a lot of

talk of Moss being a car-breaker then, you know, but I don't subscribe to that. I've got to say that for me Moss epitomized all the things that a race driver should be. . . . Moss . . . could get into a diabolical car and, without rebuilding it, go off and win."

Moss came closest to winning the World Championship when he won four of the ten Grand Prix races in 1958 and recorded the fastest laps on three occasions. He scored forty-one points during 1958, the best showing he would ever record, but he fell to second place. Moss knew that his opportunity for the championship had passed and the title seemed just a little less important to him than the fun of racing.

By 1959, he joined whisky magnate Rob Walker's racing team, driving privately entered Coopers and Lotuses. These machines were no match for the factory works of Ferrari and Maserati, thus relegating Moss to underdog status. But his audacity on the track stunned the big boys when he raced for a first-place finish at the Argentine Grand Prix in a privately entered 2-liter rear-engine Cooper under Rob Walker. Moss covered the entire race without a single stop and finished ahead of Ferrari on bald tires.

But again, an inferior car kept Moss from taking another important race, this time at the German Grand Prix. Entering a Vanwall, Moss had a machine that was handling well when it inexplicably crapped out.

Lotus' Colin Chapman was struck with the advances the rear-engined Cooper made in 1959, and decided to attempt the same technology in his Lotus Mark 18. Built with a tubular space frame chassis and double wishbone suspension, the Lotus was underpowered with a 2.5-liter Coventry Climax engine, compared to the likes of Ferrari with 240 braking horsepower at 6750 rpm. The key to any success the Lotus may enjoy lay in the capabilities of a driver like Moss and the car's lightweight front end.

Although fragile and often fraught with mechanical problems, the 18 was nonetheless a machine to be reckoned with. In 1960, Innes Ireland drove it to top honors in the Richmond Trophy at Goodwood and Moss captured a victory at the International Trophy at Silverstone. It achieved its greatest victory when Lotus won its first Grand Prix at Monaco with Moss behind the wheel. Moss would repeat the victory in 1961.

At the Belgian Grand Prix at Spa, Moss entered another Rob Walker–sponsored 18. During a practice run, Moss was coming out of a turn at 130 mph (209.1kph) when the Lotus lost its left rear wheel, flipped, and ejected Moss, whose legs, nose, and back were broken. Moss stunned his fellow drivers by returning six weeks later to win a 75-kilometer sports car race in Sweden and drive a 19 at Karlskoga.

In 1961, he entered eight Grand Prix races, capturing two victories and recording a pair of the fastest laps. It would garner him only a third-place finish in the World Championship with twenty-one points. It also marked his last year in Grand Prix driving.

In April 1962, Moss entered a nonchampionship race at Goodwood in another Lotus. Moss had passed driver Graham Hill on the left when he left the track and plunged at what appeared to be full throttle into a bank without attempting to brake or spin out. The front of the very light, tubular-framed Lotus folded in half. Moss was trapped in the car for 40 minutes. He later remembered nothing of the crash or the events leading to it. Moss suspected that the front suspension or steering failed, but never knew for sure what really went wrong.

After lying in a coma for four weeks, Moss woke up at Atkinson Morely Hospital to discover that he was partially paralyzed on his left side. He would remain paralyzed for another six months.

In May 1963, a recovering Moss returned to Goodwood with a Lotus Mark 19 for a test run, only to discover that his concentration and instincts were shot. He drove well based on his experience, but while driving he had to give conscious orders to himself to brake or downshift on a turn. "I used to look at the rev counter without taking my eyes off the road," he once said. "Not only that, I could see the rev counter and the road and a friend waving to me, all at the same time. . . . I've lost that. That's gone."

Moss retired immediately. After another year passed, he believed everything had come back to him; nevertheless he elected to remained retired.

Although Stirling Moss never won the World Drivers Championship, that elusive prize pales when one considers Moss' awesome record on the track. He raced in sixty-six Grand Prix races altogether and captured sixteen first-place honors—making him perhaps the greatest driver never to win the championship.

CHAPTER FIVE

CORVETTE

Recognizing that the European automakers were carving a niche in the sports car market in the United States, Chevrolet decided to test the waters with a fiberglass-bodied 6-cylinder two-seater.

It almost failed.

Debuting in 1953, the Corvette was based on the EX-122 show car that toured the United States in the 1952 Motorama. It was one of very few Motorama show cars that actually got into production with its original styling almost entirely intact.

Sports car enthusiasts who were keeping an eye on Detroit's foray into the market were disappointed on several fronts after the first Corvette rolled off the assembly line in Flint, Michigan, on June 30, 1953. First, Chevrolet was the maker of uninspiring blue-collar family cars built for mule work, for running errands to the market, and for taking the kids to school. So even the source of the new sports car was somewhat suspicious. Second, the Corvette featured a 235-cubic-inch inline 6-cylinder engine that generated a modest 150 braking horsepower at 4200 rpm. To make matters worse, it came with a Powerglide automatic transmission. Comfort was minimal, which wasn't necessarily a bad thing, but the new car lacked such basic amenities as roll-up windows, a heater, and an AM radio.

The saving grace, however, was its strikingly handsome looks. The Corvette featured clean, no-nonsense styling, a remarkable departure from the usual Detroit fare. It had rounded front fenders with recessed headlamps, a chrome-framed grille with thirteen vertical chrome bars, a wraparound windshield, and bullet-shaped taillights integrated into the rear fenders. Sitting on a 102-inch (259cm) wheelbase, its overall length was 167 inches (424.1cm).

Minor changes were made throughout the production run, which moved from Flint to St. Louis, Missouri, later in the year. Sales were nearly disastrous, with only three hundred units sold the first year. Although the Corvette was virtually unchanged for the 1954 model year, sales picked up considerably. However, sales figures were still far below Chevrolet's projections with 3,640 units built.

Chevrolet brass believed they had hit a crisis point for the 1955 model year and were unsure as to whether to continue production of the Corvette. But Ford introduced with great fanfare—and later with excellent sales—its two-seater Thunderbird for 1955, effectively forcing Chevrolet into competition in the sports car market. Like a redheaded cousin at the family picnic, the Corvette was here to stay, and the Chevrolet family wasn't necessarily happy about it. But the Thunderbird, in a peculiar way, revived the sagging interest in Corvette and, ironically, kept it alive. Zora Arkus-Duntov, the brilliant Corvette chief engineer, played a significant role in maintaining the Corvette by convincing GM to keep the car in production. While sales numbered only 700 that year, as many as 680 came equipped with a 265-cubic-inch V8 engine, thanks to Arkus-Duntov.

Throughout the 1950s, the Corvette continued to improve in both styling and options. The year 1956 brought a totally new fiberglass body with sculptured sides, cowl ventilators, extended headlamps, tunneled taillights, and an

optional removable hardtop. The old inline 6-cylinder engine was gone and the V8 was the only power offered. While the V8 developed 210 horsepower, a specially tuned version could generate 225 with twin 4-barrel Carter carburetors and hit 60 mph (96.5kph) in 7.3 seconds. At Sebring, a production '56 Corvette won its class in the 12-hour marathon. A fuel-injected 283-cubic-inch V8 followed in 1957, but only 1,040 of the 6,339 units produced were so equipped.

A "duck tail" rear end with four cylindrical taillights were the significant changes for 1961, but the big change for the Vette followed with the 1963 model in the form of the now-famous Sting Ray coupe and ragtop. The Sting Ray was modeled after the anatomy of a shark, with flat, almost sinister lines at the front, and a tapered fastback in the rear. Styling chief Bill Mitchell, who succeeded Harley Earl in 1958, became enamored with sharks after a deep-sea fishing trip. He wanted an automobile that reflected the powerful yet graceful feeling of the shark.

The concept of the '63 Sting Ray was developed in 1959. Dubbed the XP-720 design, stylists added a split window that was reminiscent of the 1956 Oldsmobile Golden Rocket show car. Controversy swirled over the split rear window: Mitchell loved the feature, but Arkus-Duntov saw it as a visual obstruction, a gimmick with no useful purpose. Mitchell prevailed and the Sting Ray was produced with the split window, but Mitchell finally conceded to Arkus-Duntov in 1964, when the car was produced without the split.

While the split window was not a practical feature, it looked handsome and masculine and in keeping with the wedge-shaped characteristics of the car. The window has now become one of the most desirable features sought by Corvette collectors.

Buyers had four levels of horsepower to choose from, all within the 327-cubic-inch V8. The base engine offered 250 horsepower or the optional 300 horsepower version. The fuel-injected 360-horsepower 327 L84 was the top-of-the-line version, with the L76 essentially the same as the L84 but generating 340 horsepower. The wheelbase was shortened to 98 inches (248.9cm) and many options were offered, ranging from air conditioning (rarely ordered by buyers) to power brakes and an off-road exhaust system.

The first major restyling change since the 1963 model came with the '68 model. Gone was the fastback and in its place was the tunneled-roof T-top and removable back window. The front end was a logical progression from the 1963–67 models, but was more aerodynamic and sloped lower to the ground. The rear deck was shorter and blunter, and contained four round taillights that would become a Corvette trademark for the next two decades.

A 1998 Corvette pays homage to the road-sters of yesteryear with its slightly bulbous lines, yet still adheres to the shark-like quality of more recent generations.

Arkus-Duntov, who would gain a reputation as "Mr. Corvette" or the "Godfather of the Corvette," was largely responsible for the vast array of powerplants offered during the muscle car years in Detroit. He belonged to the engineering brain trust under GM president Ed Cole at Chevrolet, and his engineering feats during his tenure at Corvette were legendary.

Arkus-Duntov's L88 engine was not designed for the streets, but in order to satisfy homologation requirements of

SCCA racing, it had to be offered to the public. Chevrolet made the engine available to the public, but took many steps to make it as unappealing as possible to the average buyer. The L88 was offered only in models without heaters or radios. Factory literature listed the 427-cubic-inch engine as generating 430 horsepower, but actual output was 530; the same literature listed torque at 485 lbs.-ft. at 4000 rpm, but it was probably much higher with a 12.5:1 compression ratio. It could hit 60 mph (96.5kph) in 6.8 seconds and covered a quarter mile (402.3m) in 13.6 seconds at 111 mph (178.5kph). Chevrolet's attempts to limit the L88's public appeal were successful: a paltry 20 L88s moved out of the factory in 1967 and just 116 were sold for the 1969 model year.

Arkus-Duntov specifically designed the L88 for racing, and its high idle at 2000 rpm, rough ride, and inadequate

cooling system for street use made it a poor choice for daily transportation. But its near-top speed of 200 mph (321.8kph) made for a very exhilarating ride nonetheless.

For the 1973 model year, Arkus-Duntov had hoped for a Corvette that would take its cue from the masters of rear- and mid-engine design—those European automakers that produced Lotus, Ferrari, Maserati, and others. It was Arkus-Duntov's dream to produce an all-aluminum mid-engine Corvette, which would be a radical departure from anything that Chevrolet had considered since the Corvette was born in 1953.

General Motors had intended to produce the Wankel rotary combustion engine in 1970. It had planned a 2-rotor version of the engine for the Chevrolet Vega, and Cole made preliminary plans for a 4-rotor mid-engine version for the

Corvette. An all-new body design was incorporated that featured gullwing doors. This version, featuring the 4-rotor engine, was introduced at the Paris Salon in 1973. It was a clean, sleek design that foreshadowed future Corvette styling. However, the project had to be abandoned due to high emissions and poor gas mileage. Planning for an alternative mid-engine design limped quietly along until 1978, when Chevrolet gave up because of the car's impracticality. This time, the new model was done in by severe limitations in passenger and luggage space.

Arkus-Duntov attempted to revive the proposal in the early 1990s without success. He died on April 21, 1996, without achieving his last dream.

Arkus-Duntov's street machines endured even without some of his more forward-thinking ventures being realized. The 454-cubic-inch V8 proved immensely popular before being dropped in 1975. The convertible was discontinued as well from 1976 through 1985. And despite oil shortages in 1973 and 1978, sales remained relatively healthy,

peaking in 1979 with 53,807 Corvettes produced. And 1984 saw 51,547 roll off the factory floor.

The fourth-generation Corvette appeared in 1984 and featured improved visibility and aerodynamics. Corvette stylists eschewed the flashiness found on many new offerings from competing sports car makers and focused on a clean, streamlined model with a lower roofline.

The massive clamshell hood blended easily with the integral front fenders, and access was improved to both the engine compartment and the front suspension. Vette designers could better display the engine compartment, which featured a magnesium air cleaner cover, a functional T-handle dipstick, and aluminum control arms. Designer Jerry Palmer confessed that he spent as much time designing the engine compartment as he did the exterior.

The fifth-generation 1997 C5 Corvette harkens back to its roots and the styling of its competitors of an era gone by. This retro look maintains many of the characteristics that made Corvette the leading sports car in the United States,

although it features gently rounded front fenders that don't overstate the yesteryear look but pay it subtle homage. It sits on a 104.5-inch (265.4cm) wheelbase with an overall length of 179.7 inches (456.4cm).

Under the hood is a 5.7-liter LS1 V8 engine with sequential fuel injection. An electronically controlled 4-speed automatic transmission (or optional 6-speed manual) transfers the power to the rear wheels. The engine provides 345 braking horsepower to generate 350 lbs.-ft. of torque.

The Corvette plant moved from St. Louis to Bowling Green, Kentucky, in 1981 and saw its 750,000th car built there on October 26, 1983, and its one millionth on July 2, 1992. Through June 30, 1994, 1,044,000 Corvettes were produced, including 277,023 convertibles.

The genius of Arkus-Duntov. The birth of the Ford Thunderbird. Performances at Sebring. The 1963 Sting Ray. The C5. These milestones gave Corvette a long life when a skeptical public, fierce safety and environmental regulations, and fuel shortages conspired to kill it.

Corvette Sports Coupe (1968)

SPECIFICATIONS

Weight — 3,055 lbs. (1,386.9kg)

Tire size — F70 × 15

Engine type — Overhead-valve V8

Bore and stroke — 4.00 × 3.25 in.

Displacement — 327 cu. in.

Compression ratio — 10.0:1

Carburetor — Rochester Type 4MV 4-barrel

Braking horsepower — 300 @ 5000 rpm

Transmission — 3-speed manual (standard)

DIMENSIONS

Wheelbase — 98 in. (248.9cm)

Length — 182.5 in. (463.5cm)

Front tread — 58.7 in. (149cm)

Rear tread — 59.4 in. (150.8cm)

PERFORMANCE

0–60 mph (0–96.5kph) — 7.7 seconds (L-79 engine option only)

0–100 mph (0–160.9kph) — 20.7 seconds (L-79 engine option only)

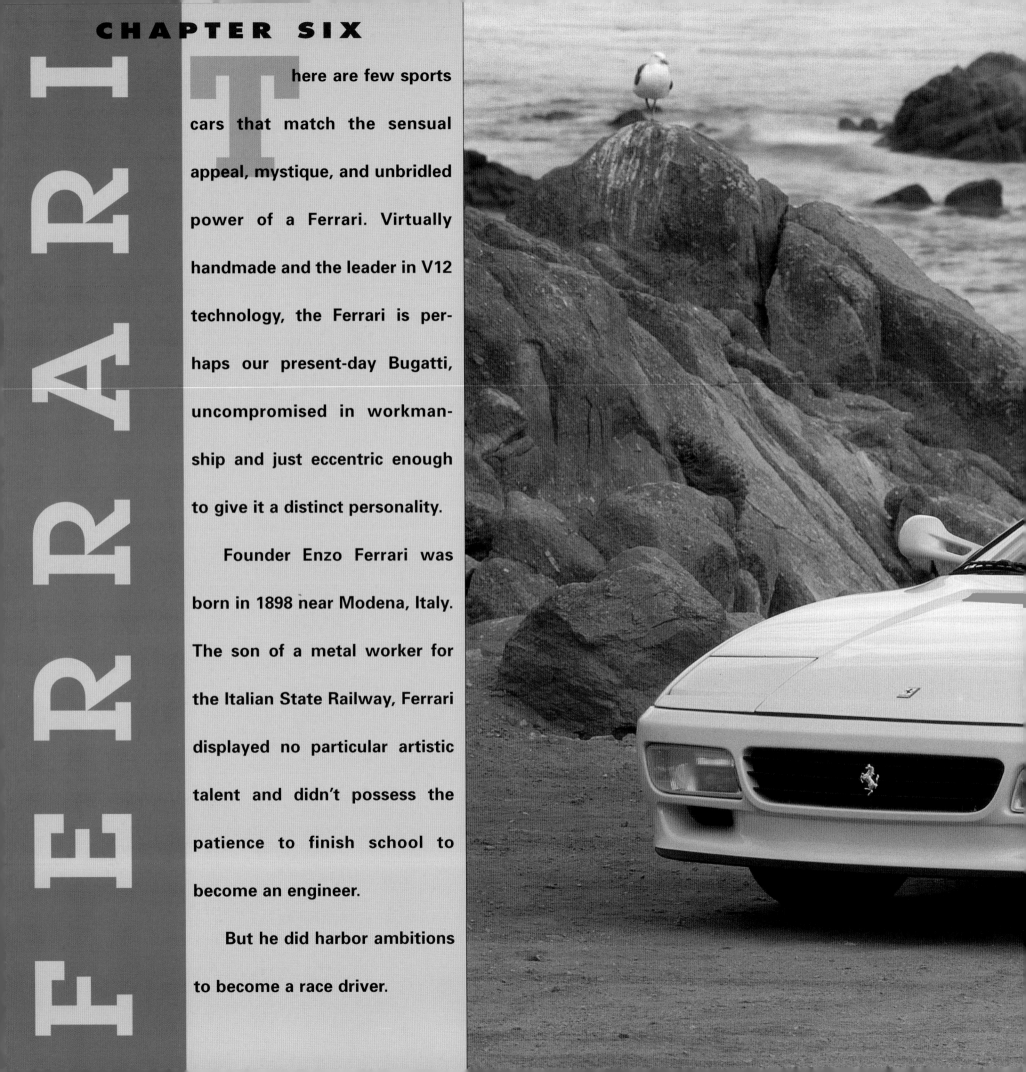

CHAPTER SIX

FERRARI

There are few sports cars that match the sensual appeal, mystique, and unbridled power of a Ferrari. Virtually handmade and the leader in V12 technology, the Ferrari is perhaps our present-day Bugatti, uncompromised in workmanship and just eccentric enough to give it a distinct personality.

Founder Enzo Ferrari was born in 1898 near Modena, Italy. The son of a metal worker for the Italian State Railway, Ferrari displayed no particular artistic talent and didn't possess the patience to finish school to become an engineer.

But he did harbor ambitions to become a race driver.

After World War I, Ferrari became acquainted with Ugo Sivocci, a test driver for auto maker CMN (Costruzioni Meccaniche Nazionali). Sivocci hired Ferrari as his assistant. Before long, Ferrari was racing for a living. In 1919, he finished ninth in the Targo Florio. Later he took third place in a hill climb.

By 1920, he had become a test driver for Alfa Romeo and had placed in several Targa Florio races. He never achieved greatness as a race driver; most of his best driving was limited to obscure hill climbs and races at the local level. Still, his association with Alfa Romeo was beneficial to him in many ways. Despite his mediocre talent on the racing circuit he climbed the company ladder, becoming closely associated with sales manager Giorgio Rimini, who also directed the company's racing program.

During his tenure at Alfa Romeo, Ferrari's biggest coup was bringing Vittorio Jano over from Fiat. Jano soon proved to be invaluable, designing a new car to beat Fiat.

Ferrari remained with Alfa Romeo until 1938; at one time he even headed the company's racing program. But he quit in a huff after arguing with the managing director, Ugo

Gobbato, over personnel issues. Now Enzo Ferrari was on his own. But he had been frugal with his money through the years with Alfa Romeo, and had cultivated many wealthy friends who were now willing to invest in a new company.

He formed Società Auto-Avio Costruzione Ferrari, ultimately developing a pair of 1500-cc cars known as 815s. After the war, Ferrari, joined by Enrico Nardi, began building sports and racing cars; together they established a small plant in Maranello, near Modena. They developed a 1500-cc V12 engine that was designed by Gioacchino Colombo. First out of the gate was the Tipo 125, Tipo meaning "Type" and the number 125 denoting the cubic capacity of individual cylinders; this would become a consistent identification number for virtually all later Ferraris.

While the Type 125 was a milestone car for the young automaking company, it was the Type 166 Sports V12 that ignited the Ferrari myth. Only two of the notchback coupes were built. Both featured a 1995-cc engine with aluminum alloy block and heads for a braking horsepower of 110 at 6000 rpm. A convertible, however, was entered in the April 1948 Targo Florio road race. Driven by Clemente Biondetti,

the convertible captured first place, then took top honors again a month later at Mille Miglia.

It was an auspicious start for Ferrari. The Type 166 would be produced between 1948 and 1951, with the Type 195 and the Type 212 beginning production in 1950.

Ferrari's V12 had a single overhead camshaft for each bank of 6 cylinders. Each bank had its own distributor and fuel pump. Acceleration was extremely sensitive to the touch of the foot, and it wasn't uncommon for a driver to blow an engine by overrevving while missing a shift on the 5-speed manual transmission. Hitting 6000 rpm was okay for maximum use of horsepower, and even 8000 rpm was good for very brief bursts of acceleration.

This sensitive machine gave novice drivers fits, and its performance and well-being were jeopardized if it was over-revved. The V12 required a sensitive throttle and excellent coordination in shifting from one gear to another.

Ferrari enjoyed a honeymoon period in the years immediately after the war by winning many racing events. That came to an end in 1950 when Alfa Romeo put up its

Alfetta, which outdistanced all of its competitors. Other automakers—Jaguar, Aston Martin, and Lancia among them—were also making inroads on the racing circuit. Ferrari continued to make refinements in both engine and chassis design to meet the challenge. A 2.3-liter sports model took the 1950 Mille Miglia.

Ferrari also began developing a 3.3-liter model, but the transmission from previous models couldn't handle the pressure and it failed. When the initial problems were resolved, the 3.3-liter engine provided the basis of Ferrari's Formula One race car. It also proved to be the engine that would beat the Alfas. At this time, the "America" models were produced that allowed Ferrari to offer a Grand Prix racing car, sports car, and standard passenger model.

The Type 340 America, sitting on a 95-inch (241.3cm) wheelbase, served as the foundation for the evolutionary Ferrari. Its V12, initially based on the very successful 3.3-liter model, was designed by Aurelio Lampredi. It featured an aluminum alloy block and heads, and displaced 4101 cc. It could reach 60 mph (96.5kph) in about 6 seconds with a top speed of more than 145 mph (233.3kph), thanks to 280 braking horsepower.

The 340 America was introduced at the Paris Salon in October 1950. Three months later the 342 America was born.

It sat on a longer wheelbase of 104 inches (264.1cm). Only six 342 Americas were built for competition and to complement the 340.

The Type 250 Europa followed, but only seventeen of them were produced during 1953–54. The big news from Ferrari, however, was the introduction of the Type 250 GT. Although only about twenty-five hundred of them were manufactured, it marked the first time that Ferrari issued a true production model—even if production was somewhat limited. The type 250 GT sat on a 102.3-inch (259.8cm) wheelbase with a large-diameter, ladder-type tubular frame. Other GT models—the California, GTO, and GTB—came with 94.5-inch (240cm) wheelbases.

The V12 for the Type 250 GT came equipped with a 2953-cc displacement with braking horsepower of up to 220 at 7000 rpm. Top speed was 155 mph (249.3kph).

Through the 1960s, Ferrari offered a succession of GT models, including the 250 GT Berlinetta Lusso. In 1961, Ferrari captured the 1-2-3-4 positions with its 250 GT Berlinettas. The company had also been experimenting with mid-engine race cars since 1960, but there was limited success on the track. When one model caught fire at Sebring, it was destroyed and plans for such racing machines were scrapped.

During the early years of mid- and rear-engine technology, Ferrari was by no means a leader in the field. Porsche began to emerge as a strong competitor in the racing field with its rear-engine design. Rear- and mid-engine technology made cars lighter and allowed for more aerodynamic body design. Ferrari was content to let other automakers devote huge amounts of money and research time to mid- and rear-engine development. When Ferrari was ready, he would take the engine and perfect it to Ferrari standards. It's been said that Ferrari never had an original idea, but the fact remains that when he seized someone else's concept, he would eventually improve or even perfect it.

In 1956, Enzo Ferrari's beloved son, Dino, died at the age of twenty-four. He had suffered from a lifelong illness and the exact cause of his death remains a mystery today. A

grief-stricken Ferrari went into seclusion, but eventually emerged to honor his son by naming a new and unique car after him. The first was the Dino 206 GT. With its V6 engine, it was an unusual effort for Ferrari. The Dino was very much a separate line for Ferrari—it did not carry the Ferrari name or the prancing black horse emblem. The engine, in fact, was built by Fiat.

Its body, by Pininfarina, was striking. It was low with only a 49.3-inch (125.2cm) height on a short 90-inch (228.6cm) wheelbase. Its lines were curvy, almost flamboyant, with its headlamps set deep into front-fender nacelles. A very small horizontal grille—a slit, really—opened at the sloping nose. Under its hood was a 1987-cc engine with

braking horsepower of 180 at 8000 rpm. Performance, especially for this modest V6, was excellent—a flat 7 seconds for 0–60 mph (0–96.5kph) with a top speed of 142 mph (228.4kph). About 150 Dinos were produced in all.

The Dino would remain in various incarnations through the mid-1970s—including the 308 GT4 that featured Ferrari's first mid-engine V8 for road cars—before being replaced by the Mondial 8, another V8 model.

In the mid-1980s, Ferrari expanded its range of power options to his V8s and V12s. Although he was in his eighties, Enzo Ferrari still supervised the marque's racing program, winning the Constructors title in 1982 and 1983. He continued to help design new Ferraris until he died in the spring of 1988 at the age of ninety.

With the debut of the Testarossa in late 1984, Ferrari had produced a model that became as synonymous with the thrill of driving as the name Ferrari itself. Even the name Testarossa, which means "redhead," evoked a mysterious, fiery power. It was a different two-seater for Ferrari—flatter and somewhat more square than the Berlinetta or the Dino—but its slick and fluid lines gave the feeling of moving even at a standstill.

Designed by Pininfarina, the shape of the Testarossa was fine-tuned in a tunnel to focus on front and rear downforce. The body was constructed of a combination of aluminum and steel: the fenders, the hood, and most of the rear were fabricated from aluminum, while steel was used to reinforce the roof and doors. Six large horizontal ribs graced the bodyside, stretching from the front of the doors into air scoops at the rear quarter panels. The twin rear scoops fed air into twin radiators behind the cockpit. Compared with previous editions of Ferrari, this car had a broader, more muscular look, thanks in large part to the rear tread dimension that was nearly 6 inches (15.2cm) wider than the front tread. With a 100-inch (254cm) wheelbase it was longer than the Mondial, but the Testarossa was more than 5 inches (12.7cm) lower at 44.5 inches (113cm) in height compared with Mondial's 49.6 inches (125.9cm).

Under the hood the Testarossa was equipped with a horizontally opposed, twin-overhead-cam 12-cylinder engine that featured 48 valves and was very similar to Ferrari's Berlinetta boxer model. The 4942-cc displacement allowed for an 8.7:1 compression ratio for 380 braking horsepower at 5750 rpm. The torque could be breathtaking with

354 lbs.-ft. at 4500 rpm. It was a machine that hit 60 mph (96.5kph) in 5.3 seconds, pinning the driver deep into the leather-upholstered bucket seat. Top speed was not for the faint of heart: more than 180 mph (289.6kph), and that's for a standard road car.

Rivaling the Testarossa in popularity among the rich and even exceeding the Testarossa in price (costing up to three times the price of the $135,000 Testarossa) was the F40, a V8-powered virtual race car that hit European roads in 1987. The expensive racer was only a distant dream for Americans—only a handful of them could afford it, and they still had to wait for the car to become certified for sale in the U.S.

Conceived partially in response to the supercar Porsche 959, the F40 was also intended to mark Ferrari's fortieth anniversary and give customers a street-legal car that came as close to a race car as possible. It featured a tall airfoil in the rear as well as wheels and tires that rivaled the top Indy cars in width.

The cockpit was amazingly stark, but very much in keeping with its racing aspirations. There were no door panels, no carpeting, no roll-up windows, and no distracting radio. Plexiglas panes were used instead of glass, and seats were upholstered not in the expected leather but in Day-Glo orange Nomex. Both seats also featured a four-point safety harness. The car possessed many of the characteristics of Ferrari's Evoluzione, GTO, and 308/328 models. The F40 had the same wheelbase as the GTO—96.5 inches (245.1cm)—and the same height as the Testarossa. The chassis was fabricated as a steel-tube space frame, and the body was built from composite materials reinforced with carbon fiber and Kevlar.

The F40 proved to be a terror on the road for which amateur drivers needed not apply. It was powered by a 32-valve 2936-cc engine, which is surprisingly small for the monstrous braking horsepower of 471 at 4000 rpm and outlandish 426 lbs.-ft. of torque. Ferrari claimed that the F40 could exceed 200 mph (321.8kph)—a figure few owners would dispute—and it could go from 0 to 60 mph (96.5kph) in just 3 seconds. If that didn't satisfy the suicidal driver, an optional kit could be installed to boost braking horsepower to 671. Only four hundred cars were built during the first year of production.

Ferrari initially had difficulty getting the F40 certified for U.S. sale. In fact, European customers could have one for as little as $180,000, but U.S. buyers could expect a price tag approaching $400,000. And those were financially "qualified" customers, according to Ferrari standards.

With the exception of the Lamborghini of today—which was designed specifically to compete against Ferrari—and the Bugatti of yesteryear, there is no other sports car on the road that comes close to the prestige, workmanship, and virtual eroticism of high-performance driving than the Ferrari. Pininfarina set the design standards for Ferraris and, ultimately, for all European sports cars. Ferrari was extremely careful with its line of cars, demanding handmade bodies and building only one engine per day to ensure quality and performance.

Ferrari Dino 246 GT (1973)

SPECIFICATIONS

Weight — 2,380 lbs. (1,080.5kg)

Tire size — 205/70VR14

Engine type — Dual-overhead-cam "Vee" type 6-cylinder

Bore and stroke — 3.64 × 2.36 in.

Displacement — 2418 cc

Compression ratio — 9.0:1

Carburetor — Three Weber 40DCNF13

Braking horsepower — 195 @ 7600 rpm

Torque — 167 lbs.-ft. @ 5500 rpm

Transmission — 5-speed manual

DIMENSIONS

Wheelbase — 92.1 in. (233.9cm)

Length — 165 in. (419.1cm)

Height — 43.9 in. (111.5cm)

Width — 66.9 in. (169.9cm)

Front tread — 56.1 in. (142.4cm)

Rear tread — 56.3 in. (143cm)

PERFORMANCE

0–60 mph (0–96.5kph) — 8 seconds

Top speed — 140 mph (225.2kph)

JUAN MANUEL FANGIO

Postwar Europe wasted no time in establishing racing circuits from the ruins of Allied and Nazi bombing. From Italy to France and Germany to England, racetracks reemerged within months of the Axis surrender on May 8, 1945. Grand Prix racing would debut in 1948, while the World Drivers Championship, a point system for drivers in six Grand Prix races and the Indianapolis 500, began in 1950.

Prewar designs and powerplants reigned supreme during those early months, with Alfa Romeos in particular dominating the circuits. And along with the aging prewar machines were aging prewar drivers who were in their final days of glory. Giuseppe "Nino" Farina, a member of the legendary Pininfarina coachbuilding family, Frenchman Jean-Pierre Wimile, and Italian Luigi Villoresi were among dozens playing out their last hand behind the wheel.

Emerging young Turks were sorely missed. The young and brash Stirling Moss was beginning to make noise, but there were few others to fill the growing void. There was one exception, however, and that came in the form of Juan Manuel Fangio, the son of a transplanted Italian house painter in Argentina. What set Fangio apart from the limited new crop of drivers was the fact that he was already thirty-eight years old when he competed in his first race in Europe. He was by no means a ladies' man, so that the adulation from the European press, female fans, and all-around racing nuts made him nervous and homesick for Argentina and his wife.

During his storied Grand Prix career between 1949 and 1957, Fangio, who cut his teeth on extraordinary mountainous dirt road races in South America, was a member of the top European teams, piloting Alfa Romeos and Maseratis, and even spent a hellish season under Enzo Ferrari's thumb.

Fangio missed a complete season when he broke his neck in 1952 in a nonchampionship race at Monaco. But before retiring at the age of forty-five, Fangio secured five World Championships ('51, '54, '55, '56, and '57) and twenty-four Grand Prix victories. Many of his records have been eclipsed over the years, but no driver since has achieved Fangio's level of success in so few races.

Born in 1911 in Balcare, a small town some 200 miles (321.8km) from Buenos Aires, Fangio was the fourth of six children. When he was ten years old, he found work in a garage. Eight years later, he was racing old Ford and Chevrolet V8s that he had modified himself. His first professional race was in a Ford taxi. Fangio and his codriver removed the body, tortured it over dirt roads at high speeds, then replaced it and returned the taxi to service on the streets of Balcare.

Fangio's physical endurance late in his career was probably a result of his grueling training in many of the Argentinian races before World War II. In 1940, he raced in the Gran Premio del Norte, which covered 5,920 miles (9,525.2km) from Buenos Aires up through the high reaches of the Andes to Lima, Peru. It was a thirteen-day trek over some of the most difficult mountain dirt roads in the world. Drivers were not permitted mechanics, so Fangio and his codriver performed all their repair work on their own, in only one hour at the end of each stage of the race. It was races like these—unheard of today—that taught him to endure physical punishment by pacing himself and his car over long periods of time.

Fangio's exposure to European racing came in 1948, when he entered a series of races sponsored by the Argentine Auto Club. The club purchased two 1.5-liter Maserati 4CLs. Fangio was assigned to drive one and performed well. He caught the attention of dictator Juan D. Perón, who was intent on

establishing Argentina as a worldwide racing force. Perón wanted Fangio to go to Europe, and with him went a new San Remo 4CLT/48 Maserati. Fangio won the first four races he entered, but the competition was mediocre at best.

In June he entered the Italian Grand Prix at Monza where he faced the dreaded Ferrari team with identical 2-liter unblown

> Juan Manuel Fangio was older than most race drivers, but he was also one of the best. At the Uruguayan Tourist Commission's International Grand Prix in March 1952 he beat all comers to take first place.

JUAN MANUEL FANGIO

Ferraris. Matched against Ferrari's Luigi Villoresi, Felice Bonetto, and Alberto Ascari, the Argentine and his three competitors averaged more than 100 mph (160.9kph) over 3 hours. At the checkered flag, Fangio finished first with Bonetto coming in second and Ascari finishing third. Fangio's victory stunned the European racing community and the Italians in particular.

After the season, Fangio was glad to be at home in Argentina, sleeping in his own bed and eating the food he was used to. The attention he received after his performance in 1949 was an awesome experience for the former boy mechanic. Fame and glory, he found, were a heady experience and the risk of surrendering to its temptations was enormous. Argentina provided a restful semblance of normalcy.

Fangio returned to Europe for the 1950 season, this time for the Alfa Romeo team. Teaming with Giuseppe Farina and Luigi Fagioli, Fangio found himself behind the wheel of a 158 Alfa, a 1.5-liter voiturette holdover from 1938. His relationship with Alfa Romeo provided some of Fangio's best moments in auto racing, especially competing against Ferrari's Ascari and Stirling Moss in a number of British cars and, later, Maseratis. During the early 1950s, Ferrari was coming into its own as an unstoppable racing machine. Ferrari was a racing monolith in the making and the supercharged Alfa Romeos occupied center stage from the moment the war ended until 1951.

The 158 Alfa Romeo was not an easy machine to drive, but Fangio soon garnered a reputation for driving the most ungodly of cars and making it look easy. Perhaps he and Moss were the only two drivers during the 1950s to take the most difficult cars and make them winners.

Alfa Romeo's truly last glorious run came in 1951 at the Spanish Grand Prix in Barcelona. On a hairy course through the streets of the city, Fangio's Alfa was pitted against Ascari's Ferrari, which had a longer range with extra gas tanks, while Fangio's supercharged Alfa was getting 1.5 miles to a gallon. But in the days when tire technology was in its infancy, Fangio did have one advantage: Ascari was riding on 16-inch (40.6cm) rims that were too small to carry the extra load of gasoline. Ascari was forced into the pits every nine laps to replace his shredded tires. Dueling at speeds reaching 160 mph (257.4kph), Fangio, playing the field

like a master chess player, waited until Ascari went to the pits before picking up speed to pass the Ferrari.

Fangio won the race, and with the victory came the retirement of the 158 Alfa, a machine from another era, one in which handling, not power, won races.

When Alfa Romeo withdrew from Formula One racing, Fangio signed on with BRM. He drove a V16 and later switched to Maseratis.

During the 1952 season, Fangio boxed himself into a commitment to race at the Ulster Grand Prix at Dundrod, then turn around the next day and drive for Maserati at Monza. On the surface, it appeared that the two races could be performed with plenty of time to get from Ireland to Italy, rest, and still get in a practice run. It was perhaps the only time that Fangio's judgment was questionable. The tight schedule and weather conspired to bring on his only serious accident.

Fangio was to fly from Belfast to Milan in a private plane after racing at Dundrod, but the plane had mechanical problems and never got off the ground. Fangio took a scheduled flight to London, from where he was to catch a flight to Milan. Bad weather scrubbed the flight. Fangio hopped a plane to Paris, then attempted to catch a sleeper train, but none was scheduled for Italy. Desperate to catch the race in time, Fangio borrowed a car and drove five hundred miles (804.5km) to Milan.

Fangio always demanded plenty of rest before a race, but he threw his regular prac-

Juan Manuel Fangio, in a Maserati, typically crosses the finish line first, here at the Grand Prix Nürburgring in Germany in August 1957. He covered 22 laps in 3 hours, 30 minutes.

tice to the wind to make this one. He was well aware of the risks. Arriving at Milan just two hours before the race, he missed his practice runs and was assigned to the back of the pack. During the second lap, he punched the accelerator at 140 mph (225.2kph) too early out of turn and lost control of the Maserati. He was ejected from the car and saw trees rushing toward him before he landed on a soft patch of grass. "At that instant, I knew what it was like to die racing," he said.

The race started at 2:30 P.M. At 3:00 P.M. he lay in a hospital with a broken neck. It would be eight months before he raced again.

His concentration and ability to handle even the sloppiest machine allowed Fangio to remain accident-free through his career, with the exception of Monza. There were worse wrecks on the track than Monza. He navigated through the gruesome wreckage at the 1950 Monaco Grand Prix and managed to scrape through the deadly disaster at the 1955 Le Mans with his Mercedes-Benz. At Monaco, it wasn't even his experience, ability, and reflexes that enabled him to avoid the wreck of a dozen cars; he was leading the race and the accident occurred behind him. He was still unaware of the accident as he sped toward it on the next lap. But he noticed the crowd was different: he was leading, but no one was watching him. Instead, he was looking at the back of their heads as they looked down the track in front of him. Fangio slammed on his brakes, realizing that they were looking at the wreck.

Fangio liked driving the Maserati 250F, but decided to join Mercedes when an invitation was extended to him for the 1955 season. His first race for Mercedes was the Argentine Grand Prix in January. Preparing to race a Mercedes D-50, Fangio knew that temperatures on the day of the race would probably hit triple digits. He began preparing by cutting down on his liquid intake to acclimate himself to the heat and ensure a resistance to dehydration.

Indeed, the temperature reached about 100°F (38°C). And true to his training, Fangio managed to drive lap after lap while his new teammate, Stirling Moss, had to pull off in his Mercedes to recover from the heat. Moss returned to the track and eventually placed fourth. Fangio? Driving for three hours, he averaged 100 mph (160.9kph) and lapped the entire field.

When Mercedes withdrew from competitive racing at the end of the 1955 season,

Fangio went to Ferrari. He joined new team members Eugenio Castellotti, Peter Collins, and Luigi Musso. But Fangio found the Ferrari operation wanting. As team leader, he found his fellow drivers excellent, but he didn't like the system, particularly when he had to practically beg to get one mechanic assigned exclusively to his own car. He also didn't like the new Lancia-Ferraris. Lancia handed its cars over to Ferrari after the 1955 season, and now the Ferrari team drove Lancia-Ferraris. But there was little Ferrari to the new cars, other than in their name. The handling in these hybrid racers was less than satisfactory, as Lancias tended to be slow in response to the wheel. Still, wins in Argentina, Britain, and Germany were enough to secure Fangio his third consecutive World Championship.

In 1957, Fangio left Ferrari for Maserati and performed well throughout the season to win his last World Championship. But

Maserati was suffering from severe financial problems and bowed out of Grand Prix racing at the end of the year.

Maserati's departure from racing also signaled the end of the line for Fangio. At forty-six, racing was beginning to feel like work to him, a dangerous thing for a driver. In 1958, he raced for the last time, in a Maserati in France. He was struggling to finish the race when Mike Hawthorn sped up behind him but intentionally pulled back to allow Fangio to cross the finish line and remain unlapped for a fourth-place finish. Hawthorn's move was the ultimate measure of respect that drivers held for Fangio. He was clearly the master of the track.

After retiring from racing, Fangio joined Mercedes-Benz as president of Mercedes-Benz of Argentina. Even years after his last full race, well into his sixties, he could be found putting on incredible displays of driving prowess in sporty Mercedes.

CHAPTER SEVEN

JAGUAR

When Americans were beginning to feel the thrill of two-seater roadsters and the Big Three in Detroit were too dim-witted to recognize the potential market, Jaguar filled the gap before the likes of Corvette and Thunderbird hit the road.

The XK 120 and, later, the wildly popular XKE offered phenomenal acceleration, top speeds that would bring a wide grin to even the most jaded driver, and a low-slung, sleek look unrivaled by anything offered by any other automaker.

equipment included leather upholstery, polished walnut wood, tachometer, turn signals, wire wheels, dual electric windshield wipers, fog lamps, tool kit, and telescopic steering wheel. These models debuted in September 1945, and by early 1947 were very popular in the United States.

Even with these fine specimens of workmanship, the Jaguar was saddled with essentially a prewar car in terms of technology and design. Lyons began turning his attention to producing a thoroughly modern roadster, but wasn't ready to make any announcements or provide the public with any glimpse of a new model until it was tested and had proven itself on the track. He developed a new engine, appropriately titled "X," then had it go through several revisions with XA, XB, and XC labels and so on until the XK was ready to be dropped into a prototype.

The new car finally emerged for the 1949 model year as the Jaguar XK 120. The numerical designation indicated that it would achieve speeds of 120 mph (193kph) or better. And it did.

Lyons introduced the XK 120 at the 1948 London International Motor Show amid much enthusiastic clamor, especially among Americans who hungered for small and sporty cars rather than the elephantine buses being produced in Detroit.

Jaguar developed a 6-cylinder inline, 70-degree twin-overhead-cam engine with 3442-cc displacement, twin SU H6 sidedraft carburetors, Lucas ignition, and an 8:1 compression ratio. It generated 160 braking horsepower at 5000 rpm. Performance was nothing short of startling. The XK 120 could do 0–60 mph (96.5kph) in about 10 seconds and

PREVIOUS PAGES: An outgrowth of the famed but ill-fated XJ13, this Jaguar XJ220 race car possesses the same aerodynamic styling with side scoops and the traditional Jaguar oval mouth at the front.

TOP: A rare look at a Jaguar SS model, this one a 1938 SS100, known then as a product of the Swallow Sidecar Co. Under the bonnet is a 3.5-liter engine capable of hitting speeds of up to 100 mph.

BOTTOM: The 1954 Jaguar XK140 was the universal symbol of cool and the standard mode of suave transportation for the young playboy bachelor—at least in the movies—of the 1950s.

William Lyons was the father of the Jaguar. Lyons and the Swallow Sidecar Co., known then as the SS and now called SS Cars Ltd., started out as coachbuilders before building complete cars in the early 1930s. Lyons developed the SS1 as a coupe, convertible, and saloon. Lyons debuted the two-seater SS90 in 1935 and, in 1936, the flamboyant SS100 roadster. The SS100 was equipped with a 3.5-liter engine and could hit 100 mph (160.9kph). The Jaguar nameplate began to appear on Lyons' cars by this time, but it wasn't until after the war, when the memory of Adolf Hitler's dreaded SS troops became infamous and the SS moniker for Lyon's cars

was dropped, that the company name was changed to Jaguar Cars Ltd.

The first Jaguars to emerge from assembly plants after the war were the 6-cylinder 3.5-liter drophead coupe and the 1.5-liter Mark V saloon. Stylish with its high curved front fenders blending into the running boards and huge headlamps mounted above the fenders, the coupe sat on a 120-inch (304.8cm) wheelbase—rather long for an English coupe—and the saloon on 112.5 inches (285.7cm). Standard

hit a top speed of somewhere between 122 and 125 mph (196.2 and 201.1kph). All this and you still got a very respectable 18 to 20 miles per gallon.

Initial test runs of the car exceeded Lyons' dreams. One run clocked the XK 120 at 132.6 mph (213.3kph). At the 1950 twenty-four-hour Montlhéry race, it averaged 107.46 mph (172.9kph), then 105.55 mph (169.8kph) in a continuous three-day run at Montlhéry in 1952.

The slick two-seater sports car was low-slung on a 102-inch (259cm) wheelbase with an overall height of just 52.5 inches (133.3cm). Headlamps were integrated into the fenders and a pair of delicate bumpers graced the front, broken by a vertical grille that lifted with the bonnet. It also featured a split windshield, and later models were given air vents low on the fenders. The interior featured the usual standard equipment of leather seats, garnished rails, a tachometer, and an electric clock.

The success at Montlhéry and other racing venues prompted the automaker to satisfy demands from private owners that their own XK 120s perform in a similar fashion. Jaguar published a special booklet on how owners could high-speed tune their cars and raise the compression ratios to as much as 9:1. The booklet also discussed lightweight flywheels, dual exhaust systems, high-lift cams, bigger torsion bars, and even racing wire wheels. In addition, the company produced the XK 120M, a high-speed version of the XK 120 that was capable of 190 mph (305.7kph).

By 1951, a fixed-head coupe debuted with a walnut-veneer dashboard. The limited-production, high-performance XK 120C also made its debut the same year. This car could produce 200 horsepower thanks to a cylinder head that contained larger valves and ports, high-lift cams, and racing pistons. Coupled with an extremely lightweight body and frame—with a curb weight of 2,128 pounds (966.1kg) compared to the 3,000-pound (1,362kg) standard models—the XK 120C could hit 143 mph (230kph). Only fifty-three Type C racing and production models were manufactured.

The XK 140 debuted in 1955. It was similar in appearance to the XK 120, but with more chrome and a redesigned chassis, larger torsion bars, and new rack and pinion steering. Along wth the new model were the XK 140M and the XK 140MC, updated versions of the performance models.

It seems that everything William Lyons did in the 1950s led to the XKE, which made its dramatic introduction at the New York International Auto Show in April 1961. The XKE was unlike anything that Lyons had developed until then. Styling was similar to the XK 120 D-Type. It was also similar to the hairy full-throttle racing machine, the XKSS, which debuted in 1957 and saw a limited production of only sixteen cars. The XKSS possessed many characteristics of the XKE, with the SS's curved windshield, recessed headlamps, and small, oval grille. The front and rear fenders were more flamboyant than those of the XKE, but the resemblance between the two versions is unmistakable.

The XKE was a unique, projectile-shaped, all-steel unibody shell bolted to a multitube structure on a 96-inch (243.8cm) wheelbase. The fastback coupe, with rear door or hatchback, offered a streamlined contour. In fact, the lines of the entire car were flatter than those of its predecessors. Headlamps were recessed into nacelles and a small, oval grille with a single thin chrome bar bisecting it replaced the horizontal grille from previous models.

Credit for the radical, even sensual, design belongs to Jaguar aerodynamicist Malcolm Sayer, formerly employed by Bristol Aircraft. This was the first Jaguar not designed by William Lyons, although Lyons, now awarded a knighthood, provided much input into the final product. Perhaps just as dynamic as its lines was the efficiency it projected. Sayer put the new effort through its paces in wind tunnels and used one test vehicle in the massive Farnborough tunnel. The sleek low lines proved to be not only elegant, but functional, decreasing wind resistance to increase performance.

Front suspension of the XKE was lifted from the D-Type Jaguar, and utilized slim transverse wishbones, longitudinal torsion bars, and telescopic shock absorbers. An anti-roll bar was fitted into the car as well because of its high roll center. The unique braking system utilized two independent Dunlop disc brake systems for the front and rear—this meant that if one system failed, the other would continue to function.

Under the bonnet was a 3781-cc 6-cylinder engine tuned to provide braking horsepower of 265 at 5500 rpm. It could achieve as much as 150 mph (241.3kph) in a straight line and 60 mph (96.5kph) in 6.5 seconds.

Total production for the first XKE from 1961 through 1964 was 7,820 roadsters and 7,670 fixed-head coupes. Models were shipped to the United States in 1961.

Late in 1964 a 4.2-liter engine was offered that allowed torque to get a boost to 283 lbs.-ft., compared to 245 lbs.-ft. from the 3.8-liter engine.

The 1997 XK8 Jaguar embodies many of the characteristics of earlier Jaguars, especially the XKE. The oval grille remains, as do the slightly rounded fenders that make it easy to spot as a Jaguar.

There is one now long-forgotten Jaguar that merits discussion because of its significance to the V12 Jaguars of the 1970s and Jaguar's attempts to recapture its glory days at Le Mans.

The ill-fated XJ13 is perhaps the most beautiful Jaguar ever conceived. It was also the most troubled. Jaguar had dominated the motorsports world in the mid-1950s with its XK 120 but retired from the circuit in 1956. Anxious to get back into the game, Jaguar brass gave chief engineer Bill Heynes permission to begin construction of the XJ13 body shell in December 1964. The sports car was to be ready for the Le Mans race in June 1966. It was to be Jaguar's first mid-engine car with a V12.

The V12 was designed by Claude Baily and was developed to serve as both a high-performance race engine and a production engine for private owners. It had a 4994-cc engine displacement with a 10.4:1 compression ratio to develop 502 braking horsepower at 7600 rpm. Its torque, however, was less than satisfactory, achieving only 386 lbs.-ft. at 6300 rpm. It also proved to be too complicated, bulky, and unwieldy in power to be an effective production engine. The V12 that Jaguar would produce in 1971 bore little resemblance to the XJ13 version.

Designed by Malcolm Sayer—father of the XKE design—and Derrick White, the XJ13 possessed more aircraft styling and principles than it did the sports automotive fare of the era. It sported the small, oval grille of the XKE and recessed headlamps.

Budget and time constraints conspired to keep it out of the 1966 Le Mans. Not only was the XJ13 not ready for Le Mans, but it was not even ready for any of its practice sessions. It was completed in March 1966, but bugs remained. It sat around for a year before test driver Norman Dewis and Bill Heynes finally took it out for a run on March 5, 1967. It was apparent right away that the car had a ways to go before it could be accepted for true race driving. The design and engineering crew continued working on the XJ13 on weekends, but the project was virtually dead in the water.

Finally, driver David Hobbs took it out on July 9, 1967, and established the fastest lap ever achieved on a British racing circuit, with an average top speed of 161.6 mph (260kph) and probably climbing toward 180 mph (289.6kph) on straightaways. The record stood until 1985 and served as one of the XJ13's greatest accomplishments. However, Le Mans in 1968 changed its regulations by imposing a 3-liter limit on prototypes. The XJ13 was no longer eligible.

The XJ13 would be used for periodic runs over the years by test drivers, engineers, and some of the lucky few charged with its care. But on January 20, 1971, it was badly damaged in a wreck at the MIRA proving ground following a secret filming session. Jaguar had intended to make public this secret project car. The company wasn't going to unveil the XJ13 as a racing vehicle, but as the father of the new production V12 that was scheduled to appear in the 3-Series E-Type Jaguar.

Norman Dewis was at the wheel. He had successfully finished filming when he decided to take the XJ13 for a few more laps. As Dewis came off the east banking of the track onto the level straightaway, the car sustained a catastrophic rear-wheel failure due to the deterioration of the wheel's

magnesium alloy. The XJ13 slid off the track into the soft mud of the infield and flipped over several times. The unibody construction of the XJ13 saved Dewis' life.

The damage to the car appeared to be terminal at first, but it was discovered later that the damage was confined to the outer shell and suspension. The unibody frame had been twisted by barely 0.06 inch (1.5mm). Jaguar still possessed the body formers to allow repairs. Two years later, Jaguar chief executive "Lofty" England gave permission to rebuild the XJ13.

A new shell was produced and the suspension was replaced, with the running gear refurbished and reassembled. In July 1973, the XJ13 returned to the track, this time at Silverstone, and performed very well.

Similar in name only to the XJ13's planned offspring, the V12, was the 1971 XKE 3-Series V12. It was the next-generation Jaguar and the first all-new engine since the debut of the XK 120. The V12 engine was featured in the convertibles and 2-plus-2 coupes. The bonnet featured a huge bulge, giving away its V12 status and hinting at the massive power underneath.

This V12 had a 60-degree overhead-cam 12-cylinder engine with a 5343-cc displacement and a 9:1 compression ratio. Braking horsepower was measured at 314 at 6200 rpm. It was modest by the XJ13's standards, but torque was 349 lbs.-ft., more impressive given the horsepower output. The production V12 allowed Jaguar to join Ferrari and Lamborghini as the only cars offering V12 powerplants.

In 1974, Jaguar discontinued the XKE coupe. That model year was also the last for the convertibles. Two new coupes, an XJ6 and XJ12, debuted the following year, but another new sports car wasn't offered until 1976.

Jaguar XKE Roadster (1961–1962)

SPECIFICATIONS

Weight —2,464 lbs. (1,118.6kg)

Tire size —6.40 x 15

Engine type —Inline, dual-overhead-valve 6-cylinder

Bore and stroke —3.425 x 4.17 in.

Displacement —3781 cc

Compression ratio —9:1

Carburetor —Three SU sidedraft

Braking horsepower —265 @ 5500 rpm

Torque —260 lbs./ft. @ 4000 rpm

Transmission —4-speed manual with optional overdrive

DIMENSIONS

Wheelbase —96 in. (243.8cm)

Length —175.3 in. (445.2cm)

Height —48 in. (121.9cm)

Width —62.3 in. (158.1cm)

Front tread —50 in. (127cm)

Rear tread —50 in. (127cm)

PERFORMANCE

0–60 mph (0–96.5kph) —6.5 seconds

Quarter mile (402.3m) —14.8 seconds

Top speed —150 mph (241.3kph)

CHAPTER EIGHT

JENSEN

Proving that some of the best sports cars to emerge from England come from small companies, the Jensen brothers' experimentation with fiberglass long before it became common and their association with Donald Healey produced some of the most innovative roadsters ever to hit the European and American markets.

Although financially troubled by the early 1970s, the Lotus-powered Jensen-Healey gave sports car enthusiasts a dynamic car at a relatively modest price before the firm permanently closed its doors in 1976.

The Jensen boys, Alan and Richard, were born and raised in Moseley, England. Neither Alan, born in 1906, nor Richard, three years younger, had any particular interest in school, and both actually did quite poorly. Richard—who would have a great aptitude for the mechanics and design of automobiles—preferred doodling car designs to doing his homework, and his attention span as a child was rather short. He usually found himself at the bottom of the class while he pursued his own interests in amateur radio and birds' eggs.

As young men, Richard found a job at Wolseley Motors and Alan took a job as an apprentice at Serck Radiators. The brothers pestered their father to buy them a car and soon found themselves with a 1923 Austin Seven Chummy. Instead of tearing up the roadways the day they got it, the boys took it home and disassembled it down to the chassis. They then rebuilt the Austin as a boat-tailed two-seater with motorcycle-style fenders. They dubbed it the Jensen Special Number One and took it to a hill climb at Shelsley Walsh, where they performed well among the more experienced and professional drivers. A short while later, they encountered Arthur Wilde, chief engineer of the Standard Motor Company, who was impressed with the Jensens' creation. He asked Richard and Alan if they would build a two-seater roadster on a Standard Nine chassis.

They agreed to produce one and developed the Jensen Special Number Two. Like Number One, it was boat-tailed with motorcyle-type fenders and a striking V-fronted radiator that Alan designed and built at Serck Radiators.

The Jensens' relationship with Standard and the subsequent publicity the Jensen Special Number Two garnered in the local automotive press led them to Avon Bodies, a Warwick-based coachbuilder. Avon asked the brothers to produce a new body for a production model, supervise its construction, and road test it. The Special Number Two served as a prototype for the Avon Standard two-seater and drophead coupe.

But the Jensens were determined to establish their own motor company. They first took over the directorship of W.J. Smith & Sons, a small coachbuilding company. In 1934, they took complete ownership of the company, christened it Jensen Motors Ltd., and began creating bodies for Morris and Wolseley, among other carmakers.

Again, the Jensen boys caught the attention of an admirer of their ingenuity. This time it was American movie star Clark Gable, who shipped them a Ford chassis to be fitted with a low-slung Jensen body. The custom car featured a modified Ford V8 engine and chassis. Before the car was to go to Gable, it was exhibited at the 1934 Ford Motor Show at London's Albert Hall. Copies of what became known as the

"Gable car" began to appear in the English countryside and became so popular that the Jensens produced 2.5- and 3.5-liter versions. Edsel Ford liked the models so much that he soon shipped Ford components to the brothers to encourage further production.

Jensen Motors would later switch from Ford V8s to Nash straight-eight engines or the reliable Lincoln V12s. When World War II broke out in 1939, the company geared up for production of military vehicles. Civilian production resumed in 1946.

The first cars off the assembly line after the war were "PW" saloons, powered by prewar 257-cubic-inch, 120-horsepower Nash engines. The Jensens had hoped to use 236-cubic-inch engines manufactured by Henry Meadows, but numerous development problems killed the plan.

The 1949 Jensen Interceptor drophead coupe would put the brothers on the map as sports car builders. Although not as flamboyant as the Jaguar or Ferrari, the Interceptor was a handsome car on a 112.5-inch (285.7cm) wheelbase with a 3993-cc engine and braking horsepower of 130 at 3700 rpm. It could hit about 100 mph (160.9kph) on straightaways, but acceleration was nothing to write home about: 12.5 seconds for 0–60 mph (0–96.5kph).

The Interceptor was well received in the automotive press, but the Jensens were after something that would revolutionize the sports car industry. They had always been interested in alternatives to aluminum or steel for building a body. They started looking for materials that could create shapes and angles on a car body and would be cheaper to produce than metalwork. Fiberglass was the answer.

Just barely beating the American-made Corvette to the punch, the Jensens constructed a body for their new four-seater Jensen 541 from reinforced fiberglass. Designed by Richard Jensen and Eric Neale, the body was assembled with three pieces. The front end of the 541 was hinged at the rear for access to the engine. The second section was constructed separately for the roof. The doors were produced in light

alloy. It was a fastback and at 105 inches (266.7cm) rode on a shorter wheelbase than the Interceptor. Its lines flowed more easily than the Interceptor's, with a striking lower profile of 53 inches (134.6cm) in total height compared to the Interceptor's 58 inches (147.3cm).

Like the Interceptor, it featured a 3993-cc 6-cylinder Austin Princess engine. Weighing as much as 612 pounds (277.8kg) less than the Interceptor, the 541 achieved better speeds, reaching as much as 112 mph (180.2kph) in a straight line and covering 0–60 mph (0–96.5kph) a tad better at 11.7 seconds.

The interior was spartan, yet comfortable. It was fully carpeted, but the transmission tunnel was unusually high. An interesting characteristic of the 541, however, was the permanent center divider in the backseat area to provide maximum comfort for two people. Unlike many four-seaters of the 1950s, Jensen provided adequate leg room for adults.

The high-performance 541R debuted in 1959 and was capable of reaching speeds of up to 125 mph (211.2kph). It featured leather upholstery, 16-inch (40.6cm) Dunlop tires on wire wheels, and a three-spoke steering wheel. The 541R was followed by the 541S in late 1960. The 541S came with a completely restyled front end. The horizontal oval mesh grille recessed under the hood gave the 541S a slightly more menacing look, especially with a mean-looking air scoop at the front of the hood.

The Jensen brothers had been producing dynamic cars since the end of World War II, so it was with considerable consternation on the part of the automotive press that they debuted their C-V8 at the Motor Show at Earl's Court in October 1962. Styled with what was dubbed the "Chinese look," it featured angled quad headlamps nacelles. While automotive design is always a subjective matter, the consensus among critics and admirers of Jensen cars was that this was a terrible misstep. Even Jensen's chief engineer, Kevin Beattie, described the C-V8 as a "styling disaster."

One car journal offered that the C-V8 was "a superb concept carefully disguised as the ugliest car in the world." If one stood at three-quarters view from the rear of the car, it

The 1974 Jensen Interceptor didn't dazzle too many buyers with its rather pedestrian styling. Blame was laid on the design-by-committee approach used by Jensen that year.

was actually quite attractive, but few sports car enthusiasts could get past the front end.

The C-V8 remained for the 1964 model year. An interesting turn to this otherwise uneventful model was the switch from a 5916-cc engine to a Chrysler 383-cubic-inch powerplant to deliver 330 horsepower. It could achieve a top speed of 130 mph (209.1kph).

The ill-fated C-V8 would last through 1966, when the Interceptor nameplate returned. First off the factory floor was a convertible code-named the P66. It was a two-door convertible that looked considerably cleaner and leaner than the C-V8. The Interceptor also marked the end of fiberglass body construction from Jensen, which now used aluminum. Designed by the Italian coachbuilder Touring, the Interceptor four-passenger saloon—the Mk I and FF models—had a roofline not unlike the Studebaker Avanti. It looked nothing like the old Interceptor and was more square with a rectangular grille, quad headlamps, and back-angled rear quarter windows. It rode on a 105-inch (266.7cm) wheelbase and still featured the Chrysler 383-cubic-inch engine with a Carter 4-barrel carburetor. Further improvements to the Interceptor included a four-wheel-drive model and antiskid braking.

In the late 1960s, Jensen suffered a series of financial setbacks. In 1967, Jensen realized that it would not be financially feasible to meet strict U.S. safety regulations. Jensen Motors, which held lucrative contracts to produce the Austin-Healey 3000 and the Sunbeam Tiger, had to sever its relationship with the two automakers. Layoffs resulted, with the workforce slashed from twelve hundred workers to four

hundred. At the same time, both brothers retired. Norwegian-born American car dealer Kjell Qvale took over the company, and Donald Healey and his son, Geoffrey, were installed on the board of directors.

The addition of the Healeys brought optimism to Jensen workers. If anything, it would put a new slant on the company and provide unlimited opportunities for new kinds of sports cars.

The Jensen-Healey merger was a dramatic change for the company. The first offering in 1972 was a smaller (92-inch [233.6cm] wheelbase) two-seater roadster with an all-steel unibody. Power was provided by a 4-cylinder 1973-cc Lotus engine with 140 braking horsepower at 6500 rpm, but the Lotus engine proved to be unreliable and hurt sales. Only 703 Jensen-Healeys were sold that first year, although the production numbers were significantly better for 1973, with 3,846 total units.

Jensen-Healey limped along, and Donald Healey dropped out of the company in 1974. The last Jensen-Healeys were produced for the 1975 model year, with a handful more turned out for 1976. The 1976 Jensen Interceptor coupe was the last in a long line of Jensens to be produced. This car, which looks similar to Studebaker's Avanti, carries only the Jensen name, but it's really a Jensen-Healey car through and through.

In August 1976, the Jensen plant shut its doors and production ended. The company went into receivership and its assets were auctioned off. Jensen Parts & Service continued to serve owners into the 1980s.

Jensen Interceptor (1976)

SPECIFICATIONS

Weight—4,040 lbs. (1,834.2kg)

Tire size—ER70VR15

Engine type—overhead-valve 90-degree V8

Bore and stroke—4.32 x 3.38 in.

Displacement—7212 cc

Compression ratio—8.2:1

Carburetor—Four-barrel

Braking horsepower—385 @ 4700 rpm

Transmission—Torque Elite 3-speed automatic

DIMENSIONS

Wheelbase—105 in. (266.7cm)

Length—188 in. (477.5cm)

Height—53 in. (134.6cm)

Width—69 in. (175.3cm)

Front tread—56.3 in. (143cm)

Rear tread—57.6 in. (146.3cm)

PERFORMANCE

0–60 mph (0–96.5kph)—7.5 seconds

Quarter mile (402.3m)—15.2 seconds

Top speed—135–142 mph (217.2–228.5.kph)

CHAPTER NINE

LAMBORGHINI

It's said that Mick Jagger bristles at the suggestion that the Rolling Stones will always remain number two in overall popularity, after the Beatles. Perhaps Ferruccio Lamborghini felt that way when his beloved namesake was inevitably compared to the legendary Ferrari. Perhaps the Lamborghini can be considered the bridesmaid, but it seems that the bridesmaid always managed to steal the show from the bride. Ferruccio Lamborghini, a longtime Ferrari owner, believed that he could build a better car. That was a pretty bold point of view, but if his critics—and, really, there were very few—say he fell short of Ferrari standards, it sure wasn't by much. His mid-engine Miura P400 and the 400 GT are among the most desirable luxury sports cars ever produced.

A relative latecomer to the sports car scene, Lamborghini was an Italian tractor and heating appliance manufacturer who made a fortune in postwar Italy. Wanting to build a high-performance car, in 1962 he purchased a plant at Sant'Agata, near Bologna. A year later, Giampaolo Dallara, who had worked for Maserati and Ferrari, joined the staff to develop a prototype and supervise the new company, which was named Automobili Ferruccio Lamborghini S.p.A. Along with Dallara came engineer Giotto Bizzarrini, another ex-Ferrari staffer.

Rather than settle for an engine that was provided by another manufacturer, Ferruccio Lamborghini insisted that his powerplant bear his own name. It was Bizzarrini's job to develop a V12 that would rival, if not surpass, Ferrari's. Bizzarrini's V12 wasn't that different from the 250 GT that

Ferrari produced for the 1964 model year, the year the first Lamborghini debuted.

The Ferrari 250 GT featured a 2953-cc engine with a 9.2:1 compression ratio and a braking horsepower output of 280 at 7000 rpm. Lamborghini's first V12 had a slightly larger displacement of 3464 cc with a compression ratio of 9:1 to deliver 280 braking horsepower at 6500 rpm. Speeds were negligible between the two marques: the Ferrari had a top speed of 124 to 155 mph (199.5 to 249.3kph) and a 6.5-second performance of 0–60 mph (0–96.5kph), while Lamborghini achieved anywhere from 137 to 161 mph (220.4

to 259kph) depending on conditions, and 7.5 seconds for 0–60 mph (0–96.5kph).

The Lamborghini V12 was installed in the 350 GTV and displayed at the Turin auto show in November 1963. The body was styled by Franco Scaglione, who had worked for Bertone coachbuilders, and constructed by Carrozzeria Sargiotto. The styling was inspired by the E-Type Jaguar and the Aston Martin DB4GT Zagato.

The prototype featured retractable headlamps, but subsequent styling changes after the Turin show made them exposed oval units. Now named simply the 350 GT, the

PREVIOUS PAGES: With enough angles to keep a draftsman busy for weeks, the Lamborghini Countach broke all the rules in sports and racing car design. Its low stance and awkwardly designed rear glass made this Lambo difficult to navigate on busy city streets.

ABOVE: A 1967 Lamborghini Miura P400 probably represents the zenith in styling for the Italian automaker, with a low profile, clean design, and a curved windshield for adequate vision.

RIGHT: A low but functional and comfortable interior of the 1966 400 V12.

redesigned machine debuted at the Geneva auto show in March 1964. Unlike later Lamborghinis, which generally featured a mid-engine design, the 350 GT had the powerplant mounted in front. It was placed on a tubular chassis, rode on a 100-inch (106.9kph) wheelbase, and stood about 50 inches (127cm) tall.

A 3.9-liter version would make an appearance only as a display model at the New York auto show in 1965. Ultimately, twenty-three of the 3.9-liter units would be built. Only thirteen 350 GTs were produced altogether in 1964 with 120 through 1967.

Two more models followed for the 1966 model year—the 400 GT and the Miura P400.

The 400 GT was basically a 2-plus-2 coupe, but the rear seats were so tiny it hardly made a difference; carrying four passengers in a 400 GT was a bit of a stretch. Looking similar but sharing no body panels with the 350 GT, the 400 GT had a higher roofline and quad headlamps. It was also equipped with a larger V12 powerplant, displacing a 3929-cc front-mounted engine with a compression ratio boosted slightly to 9.2:1 to deliver 320 horsepower.

The Miura would have the same engine, but that was now mounted amidships in the car. The V12 had a compression ratio of an impressive 9.7:1 for 350 horsepower. Marcello Gandini, formerly of Bertone, designed the body, which featured a pointed snout and sharp-edged rear and sat on a short 98-inch (248.9cm) wheelbase.

The 350 GT and 400 GT would be phased out by 1968 to make way for the Espada and the Islero. Like the Miura, Gandini designed the Espada, a front-engine model riding on a pressed-steel platform chassis on a 104-inch (264.1cm) wheelbase. It carried the same engine but was tuned to deliver varying horsepower. What made the Espada so intriguing was its very low, wide stance that gave it a distinct Indy look. It sat only 46.6 inches (118.3cm) tall and measured 71.4 inches (181.3cm) wide. The Espada had more angled lines than the graceful Miura, but that hardly mattered once on the open road, where it achieved top speeds of about 140 mph (225.2kph) and a 0–60 mph (0–96.5kph) performance of 7.8 seconds.

The Islero notchback coupe was mounted on the same tubular chassis as the 400 GT and had retractable headlamps, a long hood, and a very short rear deck. The same engine was tuned differently than in the Espada, and the 400 GT supplied the power.

A number of one-offs were produced by Lamborghini at this time. Lamborghinis were indeed rare in the United States, due to stiff U.S. safety regulations—perhaps only a dozen Miuras made it into the country. One Miura convertible was produced and featured a body made largely of zinc. Another Lamborghini, the Jota, was built by Lamborghini engineer Bob Wallace. He made his car extremely light and had a specially tuned engine that delivered 440 horsepower.

With the 1970s came the Jarama, which could hit 152 mph (244.5kph), and the Jarama S, which was capable of hitting 162 mph (260.6kph). The press liked both models' top-notch performance, but criticized their less than satisfactory ergonomics, noise, and overall ride quality. Low-speed driving also was subpar.

Designed by Gandini and placed on a short 93-inch (236.2cm) wheelbase, the Jarama was a full 10 inches (25.4cm) shorter than the Espada coupe. The same V12 3929-cc engine was featured, but this model offered a 10.7:1 compression ratio and 350 braking horsepower at 7500 rpm to generate 289 lbs.-ft. of torque.

The Urraco P250 2-plus-2 coupe was developed to compete against the Porsche 911 and the Ferrari Dino. Lamborghini announced the introduction of the Urraco in 1970, but it didn't hit the market until 1972. Instead of the popular V12, the Urraco featured a mid-mounted all-aluminum 2463-cc V8 engine. The body, by Gandini, was welded to a pressed-steel chassis and featured hidden headlamps, a pointed nose, a short hood, a raked windshield, and rear-window louvers.

Not to be outdone by Ferrari or even the Urraco, Jarama, or Espada, in March 1971 Lamborghini introduced the dramatic, even sinister-looking, Countach V12 LP400. Pronounced COON-tahsh, the name is a rather risqué Italian euphemism for an exclamation of "Good Lord!" Although it

made its entrance onto the world auto stage in Geneva in 1971, production for the European market didn't occur until 1974, and it didn't hit American shores until 1976.

By automotive design standards of the mid-1970s, the Countach was a dramatic departure from the norm. Styled by Gandini and produced by coachbuilder Nuccio Bertone Carrozzeria, it was futuristic with a liberal use of pyramids, geometric patterns, and angles. It was a design that would ultimately be copied by other European and Japanese car designers for the two-seater market in the late 1970s and early 1980s. It wasn't a sports car that appealed to everyone's tastes. In the ensuing years of production, even more angles appeared in its design, and scoops, spoilers, and other pretty accoutrements began to show up. It soon began to embody

many of the characteristics of the terrorizing machines in the horror novels of Stephen King.

The British press concluded that the Countach was the first practical futuristic car designed for mass production. It was intended to reach speeds of more than 200 mph (321.8kph), thanks to a meaty 5-liter V12 engine that generated 440 horsepower at 7400 rpm. But some compromises were made such as when the LP400 was produced with an engine used in the Miura and other Lamborghinis. Displacement dropped to 3929 cc and braking horsepower measured at 375 at 7500 rpm.

The Countach sat on a 96.5-inch (245.1cm) wheelbase and measured an extremely low 42 inches (106.6cm) from the road to the roof. Despite the smaller engine, it carried

LEFT: The 1995 Lamborghini Diablo IV carries forward the best traditions of Lambo styling and performance.

downward spiral. Immediately the company dropped its Urraco and Silhouette models, leaving the Countach as Lamborghini's only offering. Lamborghini went into receivership in 1981. It was sold to a French-Swiss company and renamed Nuova Automobili Ferruccio Lamborghini. Chrysler would purchase it in 1987.

In 1981, the company came out with the Targa-topped coupe, the Jalpa P350. Between 1981 and 1987, 410 Jalpas would be produced.

The Countach would remain Lamborghini's bread-and-butter model for fifteen years. In 1990 it was replaced by the Diablo, a V12 model capable of reaching speeds of 202 mph (325kph) and hitting 60 mph (96.5kph) in just 4.1 seconds. It offered a "cab forward" look. The 5707-cc V12 was a mid-engine model with a 10:1 compression ratio and braking horsepower of 485 at 7000 rpm.

The 1997 version of the Diablo Roadster VT appeared on U.S. shores in early 1997, but production for the American market was limited to just fifty units. Wedge-shaped with a sharp, angular silhouette and side air intakes, the Diablo is masculine and a race car in appearance in every way. The 5.7-liter 48-valve V12 engine produces 492 horsepower and a top speed just a tad over 200 mph (321.8cm). The price tag for the VT is $275,000, excluding luxury tax.

Perhaps the only drawback to the Diablo is the extremely limited rear viewing. It is, however, a work of art that can only be truly appreciated on the open road, and at a very high speed.

Lamborghini Countach LP400S (1980)

SPECIFICATIONS

Weight — 2,915 lbs. (1,323.4kg)

Tire size — 205/50VR15 front, 345/45VR15 rear

Engine type — Dual-overhead-cam "vee" type 12-cylinder

Bore and stroke — 3.23 x 2.44 in.

Displacement — 3929 cc

Compression ratio — 10.5:1

Carburetor — Six Weber horizontal 2-barrel

Braking horsepower — 375 @ 8000 rpm

Torque — 268 lbs.-ft. @ 5500 rpm

Transmission — 5-speed manual

DIMENSIONS

Wheelbase — 96.5 in. (245.1cm)

Length — 163 in. (414cm)

Height — 42.1 in. (106.9cm)

Width — 74.4 in. (189cm)

Front tread — 58.7 in. (149.1cm)

Rear tread — 63.4 in. (161cm)

PERFORMANCE

0–60 mph (0–96.5kph) — 6 seconds

Quarter mile (402.3m) — 12.9 seconds

Top speed — About 174 mph (280kph)

through many of the technical and styling features it had as a prototype. And its speed was nothing to sniff at. It was clocked at 175 mph (281.5kph) in a straight line and could hit 60 mph (96.5kph) in less than 7 seconds. The Countach was graceful in every respect, but also very masculine. The steering and clutch were very heavy and required some muscle to operate at low and moderate speeds. Only twenty-six were manufactured in its first year of existence, 1974, with sixty produced in 1975. In all, 150 LP400s were produced from 1974 to 1978.

The Countach would serve as Lamborghini's saving grace for several years as the automaker became mired in a financial morass. Lamborghini had difficulty getting its cars certified for U.S. sales, which contributed to the company's

CHAPTER TEN

LOTUS

Lotus is a unique auto-manufacturing company. It was born from the imagination of Englishman Colin Chapman, who started mass production of his cars by literally selling them in pieces.

Chapman's early efforts at developing roadsters blended sport, competition, and street-use cars. Lotus was part of a rare breed: its owners could drive a sports car to work during the week yet be competitive on the racetrack each weekend. The road car/race car hybrid proved to be just the right thing for drivers who wanted to eat their cake and have it, too.

Chapman cut his teeth on developing race cars by modifying highly tuned Ford and Austin Seven engines. His first car, built in 1948, was based on the 1930 Austin Seven saloon. This virtual prototype of the Lotus ignited a string of vehicles that would win races in its class at Le Mans, Monaco, and the Formula One Grand Prix.

Anthony Colin Bruce Chapman was born on May 19, 1928, in London and entered the University College of London at age seventeen to study engineering. In 1946, when England was suffering through a postwar car shortage, Chapman and schoolmate Colin Dare formed a secondhand car sales business. During a single year, they barely kept up with the demand of cars as customers clamored for anything that moved reliably. But by 1947, new cars were once again plentiful, and the bottom fell out of the used car market. When the business folded, a single Austin Seven saloon was the only car left in Chapman's inventory.

Using only the chassis and drivetrain, Chapman built a new body and modified the engine and suspension to develop the Mark 1. Using methods he had learned while studying aircraft construction in college, Chapman had every

body panel stressed, which added to the overall strength of the car without adding unnecessary weight. It would become the basic construction for every Lotus built.

From the Mark 1 came the Mark 2 (Chapman would use a numerical designation for his cars up to the Mark 45 in 1966). In the Mark 2 he first used an old Ford 8 engine, but soon upgraded to a 1172-cc Ford 10 and began performing well in speed trials and hill climbs.

By this time, Chapman was serving in the Royal Air Force where he became a pilot, furthering his interest in aircraft engineering and how it could be applied to automotive design and technology.

Chapman continued to tinker with one-offs, developing race cars powered by Ford engines. In 1952, he formed the Lotus Engineering Company with partner Michael Allen. Shortly after the founding of the company, the partners developed the Mark 6, their first production car. It was mounted on a 55-pound (24.9kg) steel-tube space frame covered by stressed panels of aluminum, and it had independent front suspension. It was powered by a 1099-cc 40-horsepower Ford engine with a 3-speed transmission. It was sold as a kit car—

PREVIOUS PAGES: This two-seater 1991 Lotus Elan convertible is placed on a short wheelbase to provide optimum handling on winding roads.

ABOVE: This 1954 Lotus typified Colin Chapman's initial kit-car efforts with motorcycle fenders, headlamps mounted high, and flat windscreen. This model represents early styling from the Lotus Engineering Company, founded by Chapman in 1952.

in pieces to be assembled elsewhere—to avoid British taxes on automobiles.

In 1957, Lotus began production of its cars in earnest. The Lotus Series 1 Seven debuted with a significant absence of comfort and conveniences. It was a true race car and was offered only in kit car form. It was conceived with motorcycle fenders, free-standing headlamps, a very small cockpit for the driver, and a folding windshield. It was an upgraded version of the Mark 6 with a steel-tube frame with aluminum bodywork and fiberglass nose and fenders. It would be powered by a variety of engines—Ford, BMC, and Coventry Climax—throughout its production run, but was most often powered by a British Ford 100E 4-cylinder 1172-cc engine.

It had an extremely low profile, perhaps the lowest of any sports car of the era, with an overall height of 28 inches (71.1cm), and its wheelbase was only 88 inches (223.5cm). Rack and pinion steering on later Sevens made it very quick in handling.

Still, even with its impressive good looks and roadability, it was something of a dog in performance. Top speed was 90 mph (144.8kph) and 0–60 mph (0–96.5kph) performance was only 17.6 seconds.

Also available in 1957 was the Eleven, which came in four distinct models: the Le Mans 75, the Club Le Mans 100, and two sports versions. Whatever shortcomings the Lotus Series 1 Seven had, the Eleven, especially the Le Mans 100 model, made up for it in spades. The Eleven set a world speed record for an 1100-cc car at 143 mph (230kph).

In fact, between 1956 and 1960, Lotus won a series of stunning victories not seen by any other competitor in its class. In 1956, it took first place in the 750–1100-cc class at the Le Mans 24-hour race. The following year at Le Mans it captured first in Index of Performance, the Biennial Cup, and

the 750–1100-cc class. In 1960, it took its first Formula One victory at the Monaco Grand Prix.

Late in 1957, Lotus introduced the Elite, its first closed passenger car, which used a fiberglass monocoque chassis comprised of eight box sections. The two-seater used virtually no steel body reinforcements and relied on body strength with glass-reinforced epoxide and polyester resin. Sitting on an 88-inch (223.5cm) wheelbase, it weighed in at a featherlight 1,206 pounds (547.5kg). It featured independent front suspension with coil springs and wishbones. Styling featured an oval grille low in front at the base of a sloping hood, a wraparound windshield, and a short rear deck.

It was powered by a 1216-cc aluminum 4-cylinder Coventry Climax engine. With its engine tuned to 83 horsepower, it could achieve speeds of 118 mph (189.8kph) or better and a respectable 11.1 seconds for 0–60 mph (0–96.5kph).

By now Lotuses were no longer produced as kit cars. Lotus continued to enjoy incredible success on the track. It posted one victory after another to become the winningest Formula One team between 1960 and 1981. In 1963, it entered its first Indianapolis 500 to capture second place, then came back in '65 to be the first British automaker to take first place. In 1965 alone it captured six other first-place finishes: the World Championship of Formula One

Manufacturers, the World Championship of Formula One Drivers, the Saloon Car Championship, the British Formula Two Championship, the French Formula Two Championship, and the Tasman Championship.

In the mid-1960s, Chapman developed a relationship with the small firm of Cosworth Engineering, which was owned and operated by Frank Costin and Keith Duckworth. Chapman encouraged Ford to invest in Cosworth. The result of the new relationship was the Cosworth Ford DFV engine. Jim Clark would pilot an ultralight Lotus 49 with the Cosworth engine in the 1967 Dutch Grand Prix.

Chapman also began experimenting with mid-engine models. His Type 46 Europa was the first roadable midpriced mid-engine street car. It featured a fiberglass body draped over a steel backbone chassis with a 91-inch (231.1cm) wheelbase. The Series 1 version of the Type 46 debuted in 1966 and went on sale the following year. It was first fitted

The 1964 Lotus Formula 2 race car was extremely light, if not flimsy, but thrashed the competition with the right driver. Many drivers felt it was unsafe because there was virtually no protection in a crash.

with a 1470-cc 4-cylinder Renault to generate 82 horsepower. It was later replaced by the Lotus Twin Cam engine.

Styling of the Series 1 was radical and controversial in the late 1960s. It featured tall rear panels behind the doors, something akin to exaggerated tailfins that prompted the nickname "breadvan." The front end was more traditional and very similar to the Elite with a sloping nose and recessed headlamps.

In just ten years, the Lotus became one of the top mass-produced sports cars in the world, achieving production numbers unheard of by many of its competitors. The

Series 2 Sevens, for example, hit a total production of 1,350 between 1960 and 1968. An estimated 12,224 Elans were manufactured from 1962 to 1973, and an impressive 9,230 Europas were built from 1967 to 1972.

In 1974, the mid-engine Lotus Esprit was unveiled. Low, sleek, and angular, it was designed by the Italian studio of Giugiaro Design. It was Lotus' most successful and longest-lived of the Elite, Eclat, and Esprit models. Again, like its cousins, it featured a fiberglass body with steel backbone chassis on a 96-inch (243.8cm) wheelbase. At the midsection was a 4-cylinder 1973-cc 16-valve engine with an aluminum block and head. It offered a healthy compression ratio of 9.5:1 to generate 160 horsepower at 6200 rpm. Top speed on the straightaways for the European version was 135 mph (217.2kph)—the U.S. version did 120 mph (193cm)—with a 0–60 mph (0–96.5kph) performance of 6.8 seconds.

Perhaps one of Chapman's last great achievements came in 1978, when he unveiled the Lotus Type 78 Formula

One race car. It employed "ground effects" by which it exploited the air passing beneath it to develop a downforce, of which the 78 developed more than 2,500 pounds (1,135kg). Coupled with its 1,250-pound (567.5kg) weight, it could round corners 20 to 40 mph (32.1 to 64.3kph) faster than any competing car. Also aiding its superb handling was the monocoque aluminum honeycomb chassis.

The new technology helped the Lotus 78 capture six Grand Prix titles in 1978 alone. But the ground effects technology was so astounding that by the end of the 1981 racing season, ground effects Formula One cars were banned as too dangerous.

Lotus would continue to tear up the racing circuit with win after win. By 1980, engine capacity for the Elite, Eclat, and Esprit was boosted to 2.2 liters and the chassis guaranteed for five years by the automaker.

In December 1981, Chapman died of a massive heart attack, signaling an end to an era. But Colin Chapman left a

complete electronic engine management system based on Delco components debuted in the 1989 model. It helped boost braking horsepower output to 228 and shaved almost 1 second off the 0–60 mph (0–96.5kph) performance at a 5.2-second clocking. Top speeds now reached 155 mph (249.3kph).

Despite its thrilling ride and overall popularity, the Esprit had some significant problems. It had inadequate visibility in the rear and a poor heating and ventilation system, and, inexplicably, the glare off the windshield was very distracting to the driver. The small pedals were placed too close together and there was not much headroom to accommodate tall drivers. Most of these drawbacks were corrected later, but even the early defects didn't dampen the enthusiasm of the true Lotus devotee.

The next-generation Lotus appeared in 1990 as the Elan, a moniker that returned after a seventeen-year absence. Powered by a 1588-cc dual-cam 16-valve 4-cylinder engine, its braking horsepower couldn't compare to the turbo models, but it still generated 162 horses. That same year the Turbo Esprit SE model furthered the development of an already very capable sports car. Braking horsepower was now 280, thanks largely to six fuel injectors, a deeper front air dam, and a new rear wing.

In many respects the Lotus was the little engine that could, outsmarting the marketing and engineering capabilities of the likes of Ferrari, Maserati, and Jaguar. Its long list of racing victories is a testament to its dedication to true road racing. In 1986, Lotus was bought by General Motors, but the American interest in the automaker never dampened its integrity on the track or the public street.

Lotus Esprit Turbo (1985)

SPECIFICATIONS

Weight—2,690 lbs. (1,221.2kg)

Tire size—195/60VR15 front, 235/60VR15 rear

Engine type—Inline, dual-overhead-cam 4-cylinder with Garrett AiResearch T3 Turbocharger

Bore and stroke—3.75 x 3.00 in.

Displacement—2174 cc

Compression ratio—7.5:1

Carburetor—Two Dell'orto

Braking horsepower—210 @ 6000 rpm

Torque—200 lbs.-ft. @ 4000 rpm

Transmission—5-speed manual in rear transaxle

DIMENSIONS

Wheelbase—96 in. (243.8cm)

Length—165–167.7 in. (419.1–425.9cm)

Height—44 in. (111.7cm)

Width—73.9 in. (187.7cm)

Front tread—60.5 in. (153.6cm)

Rear tread—61.2 in. (155.4cm)

PERFORMANCE

0–60 mph (0–96.5kph)—5.5 seconds

Top speed—160 mph (257.4kph)

formidable legacy that saw virtually every race car on the road assuming some part of a Lotus design or engineering achievement.

The Esprit Turbo, produced from 1981 to 1987, would be powered by a turbo engine to achieve 210 braking horsepower and a revised rear suspension and stronger chassis to handle the additional torque. The Esprit Turbo also had a deeper front spoiler and taller rear spoiler to handle the higher speeds. It managed 0–60 mph (0–96.5kph) in 5.5 seconds and 160 mph (257.4kph) in a straight line. Horsepower was boosted a bit to 215 in 1986 with a Bosch K-Jetronic fuel injection system and an increased compression ratio of 8:1. These early models rivaled the Ferrari 308GTB and the Porsche 911SC Sport.

The Esprit Turbo got a new look in 1988 when Lotus abandoned the Giugiaro design for a complete restyling. New, curvier lines and a softer look made the new version a popular car with a wider stance and more purposeful look. A

Since the start of Grand Prix championship racing in 1948, most Formula One cars have had the financial backing of the big automakers, ensuring continuing success on the track. Ferrari, Maserati, and Mercedes-Benz, to name a few, maintained a stranglehold on developing some of the premier machines ever to race a circuit. It's truly remarkable, then, that such a small fry as Lotus performed so well on the track, starting with its first win in its class in 1956 at Le Mans and continuing a formidable winning streak that would remain unbroken until 1974.

The genius behind the success of Lotus was Anthony Colin Bruce Chapman, who grew up in a middle-class area of London and believed that aircraft technology was the key to a state-of-the-art race car.

Chapman was one of the first automakers to blend sport, competition, and street cars. He developed the first successful full monocoque racing chassis, was the first to successfully use composite materials to construct a car body, developed the first Formula One four-wheel-drive vehicle, and was the first to use mid-chassis side pod radiators, which are used on all Formula One racers today. He also perfected the rear-engine race car that revolutionized the auto racing industry.

Sometimes, however, Chapman would take aircraft principles to the limit, making even his own drivers nervous about sliding into the cockpit. Lotuses were extremely light and the tubular chassis would fold like an accordion at high impact. Lightweight cars made for extremely dangerous driving, as Stirling Moss discovered in 1962 when he folded his Lotus 18 virtually in half when he struck a bank at nearly full speed.

England's war with Germany had just ended when Chapman enrolled at University College of London and began to study engineering. Like many racing enthusiasts of the era, he got his first taste of motor racing on motorcycles, traveling to and from college on a 350-cc Panther. His Panther didn't last long—he wrecked it one night on the way to a college dance, smashing it into the door of a taxi. At Christmas, however, he found himself with a 1937 maroon Morris 8 tourer.

During his freshman year in 1945 he met two people who would have a strong influence on his life: Colin Dare, who would help fan the flames of Chapman's passion in cars, and Hazel Williams, whom he would marry in October 1954. With Dare and Williams he would often amuse himself by attempting to establish speed records while finding the shortest distances between his own residence and the school, and the homes of his friend and his future wife.

England after V-E Day suffered the same automobile and fuel shortages as the United States. Virtually all nonmilitary cars on the road in late 1945 and 1946 were pre-war vintage. Fuel was still rationed. Dare and Chapman opened a small secondhand car business, selling perhaps one or two cars each week. The novice business partners often skipped lectures at school to finalize a sale. When their business expanded, they began stashing cars in a detached garage behind Williams' home. Often the pair would modify or refurbish some cars before putting them up for sale.

In 1947, the English government lifted its fuel restrictions and the manufacture of new cars began to speed up. The demand for used cars slackened, and the boys were soon out of business. The only car left in their inventory was a 1930 Austin Seven fabric-bodied saloon. Drawing on his engineering background, Chapman rebuilt the car with the chassis boxed and every body panel stressed to add overall strength without adding unnecessary weight. He would imple-

ment this philosophy of construction throughout the rest of his career.

Renaming the car the Lotus Mark 1, Chapman completed it in early 1948. He drove it to two trials, won both events, then drove it home again. He improved on the Mark 1 with the Mark 2, which was made exclusively for circuit and track use. It was initially fitted with a Ford 8 motor with an Austin Seven 4-speed gearbox, but it was not powerful enough. He dropped in an 1172-cc Ford 10 side valve engine and instantly became competitive.

He participated at the Eight Clubs, Silverstone, meeting and the Great Auclum hill climb in Berkshire in 1950. The Mark 2 was crude, but stood up well against the likes of MG and even Bugatti. It featured motorcycle-type fenders and a unique square grille with vertical bars that enclosed the headlamps.

During 1949, Chapman joined the Royal Air Force but he decided that he and the military were not compatible and left after a short stint. His exposure to aircraft technology, coupled with his engineering schooling, remained with him and would be the focus of his continuing refinement of Lotus. While deleveloping his cars, he joined British Aluminum, an engineering company, so that he could make a living while continuing with his passion.

In late 1950, a new formula car—the 750-cc Formula—was introduced for closed circuit racing. Chapman sold the Mark 2 and began to develop the Mark 3 to compete specifically in the new class. Sporting a

Colin Chapman, left, examines plans for an early edition of his famed Lotus. Chapman believed aircraft design and technology could make a better-performing race car.

chassis that weighed only 65 pounds (29.5kg), the Mark 3 was extremely light with a lean and innovative body construction. It displayed all the earmarks of what future Lotuses would be. The Mark 3 began hammering the competition race after race, and by the end of the 1951 racing season, other drivers and sponsors were inquiring about getting a copy of the Mark 3 for themselves.

Chapman focused on the weight issue, recognizing that the twin-channel chassis of the Austins, which he had relied upon for the past four years, were heavy when reinforced. Improving on the design, he developed a multitubular body frame that was light—10 pounds (4.5kg) less than the Mark 3 chassis—but extremely rigid. When he added the body panels and mounting brackets, the car tipped the scales at only 90 pounds (40.8kg). The new Lotus was powered by a brand-new Ford Consul engine that displaced about 1500 cc with a pair of SU carburetors. Williams and Pritchard Ltd. of Edmonton performed the bodywork, which featured high rounded rear wings over the wheels that formed a full valance.

When the race car debuted at the MG Car Club race at Silverstone in July 1952, orders began pouring in. The attention and accompanying prosperity allowed Chapman to quit British Aluminum and tend full-time to his automotive business.

Chapman's innovative designs and the success that followed with the Mark 6 attracted the attention of Guy Vandervell, a bearing-manufacturing magnate who developed the Vanwall race car and was a partner in BRM (British Racing Motors) as well. Vandervell shared the same dream of many Brits during the postwar period of beating the daylights out of Alfa Romeo, Ferrari, and other Italian teams. England suffered from the development of uncompetitive cars and a shortage of fine drivers. Chapman was

emerging during these early years as an answer to Great Britain's prayers and Vandervell seized the opportunity.

The Vanwall steadily improved in the early 1950s, but the car remained uncompetitive when it sidled up to the big Italian boys. Yet on several occasions, the Vanwall, driven by the erratic Harry Schell, showed promise by leading Ferrari during the early stages of some races. Vandervell was encouraged to create a three-car team for championship runs during the 1956 season.

He turned to Chapman and Frank Costin, who joined Team Lotus in 1953 as the company's technical director. Finding Costin was a stroke of good luck for Chapman, who desperately needed someone to perfect the technology in his cars. Chapman and Costin developed a light, small-diameter tubular chassis and reworked the suspension. Again Chapman and Costin based their design on aircraft principles to create a clean styling that eschewed the bulges and louvers found on most other car designs. They also recessed the exhaust pipes into the side panels and designed the cockpit to minimize airflow over the top. The design was probably one of the last great styling efforts of a front-engine racer before racing teams learned from Porsche and Cooper that rear-engine racing was the future.

The final product was one of the fastest cars on the circuit, but it was still incredibly unreliable. Stirling Moss and Mike Hawthorn, who were practically desperate to race for an English team, competed in nonchampionship races but suffered continuing breakdowns. Oddly, the unreliable Schell was making way with his new Vanwall by finishing a respectable fourth place in the Belgian Grand Prix. At the French Grand Prix at Reims, he astounded the Italian teams by leading Ferrari early in the race before blowing up his engine.

Hawthorn was driving another Vanwall and gladly gave up his car for Schell to finish the race. Again, Schell pounded Ferrari with the Chapman/Costin machine, breaking a lap record and dueling with Juan Manuel Fangio in a Ferrari for first-place honors. But toward the end of the race, the Vanwall's accelerator busted and Schell finished last.

Vanwall's performance, however, secured Chapman's place in automotive racing technology and design. While by no means a leader in rear-engine design, Chapman nonetheless saw the future of front-engine auto racing waning. After his successes with the Mark 6 and, later, the redesigned Vanwall, he built a series of front-engine cars that were simply a prelude to his revolutionary designs in 1960.

Costin helped make full use of the airflow beneath the car and developed the Mark 8 with a tubular space frame, independent front suspension, and deDion rear suspension. The car could surpass 125 mph (201.1kph) on an 85-horsepower engine. By 1955, Chapman and Costin developed another car that employed front and rear Dunlop disc brakes with an aerodynamic low drag body. Within twenty-four months of the Mark 8's debut, Lotus was producing race cars that could hit more than 140 mph (225.2kph) in 1100- and 1500-cc classes.

Chapman's Mark 18 set the racing world on its ear as one of the first race cars with a rear-engine design. Using the tubular space frame and double wishbone suspension, the 18 was grossly underpowered, with a Coventry Climax 2495-cc engine that initially generated 220 braking horsepower and, later, 240 ponies. It had difficulty keeping up with the dominant Ferraris, but in the hands of Stirling Moss and other drivers who finessed their way with superb handling, it scored a number of impressive victories, including the 1960 Grand Prix at Monaco.

The 19, successor to the 18, had a wider frame to accommodate a passenger, but still adhered primarily to the Formula One principles and design. The 18 and 19 ignited a string of wins that would make Team Lotus the winningest Formula One racing team throughout the '60s and '70s.

Again Chapman's designs started attracting attention, this time across the Atlantic Ocean. Famed American driver Dan Gurney had his finger on the pulse of European auto racing and wanted Chapman's cars on the American circuit and the Indy 500 in particular.

For the 1962 Indy 500, Gurney bought Chapman a plane ticket and brought him to Indianapolis. He gave the Brit the 25-cent tour of Gasoline Alley and had him watch the race from behind the pits. Chapman returned for the 1963 meeting with three stunning 29s. One went to Jimmy Clark and another to Gurney, with a third as a spare.

The 29 was as revolutionary as the 18. The 29 was actually based on the Type 25, the first Formula One race car to use a chassis based upon the bathtub monocoque construction. Powered by a Coventry Climax engine and weighing a mere 995 pounds

(451.7kg), it sent Jimmy Clark to fourteen Formula One Grand Prix wins and the World Drivers Championship. The 29 virtually duplicated the design of the 25, but was built with its suspension offset to the left specifically to handle the left turns at Indy. Here was a race car that basically had no chassis, but consisted of two slender aluminum gas tanks separated by the driver and joined together by an ultralight steel frame. Rather than the Coventry Climax, Chapman opted for a 256-cubic-inch Ford Fairlane V8 that generated 370 braking horsepower at 7200 rpm. While it was still underpowered compared to the rest

of the field, it weighed only 1,150 pounds (522.1kg) as opposed to as much as 1,600 pounds (726.4kg) for competing machines.

American drivers initially were not impressed. Parnelli Jones believed the fire risk was too great because what he perceived as flimsy construction wouldn't withstand impact and the tanks could explode. But Clark surprised even Lotus' greatest critics by achieving 146 mph (234.9kph) in a practice lap, then finishing second in its debut performance at Indy. Clark returned to Indy in 1965 to capture first place and silence Lotus' critics for good.

Lotus builder Colin Chapman, left, talks with driver Graham Hill, who would drive a Lotus-Ford to victory at the Grand Prix of Mexico in November 1968 in Mexico City.

When Colin Chapman died from a massive heart attack in December 1981, he left behind an indelible influence on the automotive industry, the result of a forward-thinking engineering and manufacturing philosophy that still today shapes cars designed for both racing and street use.

CHAPTER ELEVEN

MASERATI

Whenever retired race car drivers gather to tell old war stories, conversation invariably turns to the superb handling and performance of the Maserati. Equal to the racing of Ferrari and Lamborghini, Maserati evokes masculine power but civilized roadability as well.

While its acceleration performance never quite matched that of Ferrari and Lamborghini, drivers like Stirling Moss saw some models as works of art, especially in their handling of treacherous hairpin curves.

The founding of Officine Alfieri Maserati S.p.A, first at Bologna and later at Modena, Italy, was relatively late in European race car circles. The Maserati brothers didn't form their company until 1926, but they had plenty of experience in building vehicles before then.

Keenly interested in competition driving rather than road cars, Carlo, Bindo, Alfieri, Ettore, and Ernesto Maserati focused their attention on motorcycles and race cars at the turn of the century. Bindo and Alfieri served apprenticeships at the famed Isotta-Fraschini plant, with Alfieri employed as a test and race driver. Carlo had raced motorcycles, but he died in 1911 before his brothers could even think about forming their own company.

Three years after Carlo's death, Alfieri, Bindo, and Ettore formed their own company in Bologna to tune Isotta-Fraschinis into racing cars. During World War I, they turned their attention to manufacturing spark plugs for the war effort. After the war, they returned to auto racing by developing their own 4-cylinder race car and a straight-eight for another carmaker.

The company that bore their famous name was born in 1926 with the icon of their hometown of Bologna—

Neptune's trident—adopted as their company insignia. Those early years saw the Maseratis turning out a small number of twin-cam and supercharged race cars with very few for standard road driving. During this period, the Maseratis began a relationship with Diatto motorcars and built a supercharged Grand Prix car. Diatto soon fell into bankruptcy, and the race car the brothers built for the firm was returned to them. The car turned out to be the first true Maserati.

By the end of the decade—when the infant company was less than five years old—Maserati was achieving incredible success on the racetrack. The 1.5-liter Tipo 26 won its class at Targa Florio in Maserati's first serious attempt at auto racing. It then won the Italian racing championship in 1927.

Virtually all of Maserati's efforts went into race driving, but some examples of roadable cars were produced, including the 4CS-1100, the 4CS-1500, and some straight-eights, in the early 1930s.

Maserati continued to build masterful cars through the 1930s. In 1938, they sold their interest to Adolfo Orsi, an Italian industrialist, who decided to move the Maserati plant to Modena. The Maseratis remained tied to Orsi through their contract for the next nine years. The contract with Orsi

PREVIOUS PAGES: A mere sixty-one Maserati coupes and cabriolets were produced between 1946 and 1950. This 1949 coupe is powered by a 1488-cc, 6-cylinder engine and can achieve a maximum speed of about 95 mph (152.8 kph). The engine evolved from a supercharged twin-cam racing engine first built in 1936.

ABOVE: Maserati began building race cars in 1926. By the 1930s it began producing a small number of race cars that were equipped with twin-cam, supercharged engines. This 1935 model was strictly for competitive driving. Very few Maseratis at the time were built for standard driving.

expired in 1947 and the Maseratis formed their own company, Officina Specializzata Costruzione Automobili Fratelli Maserati (OSCA), at Bologna.

The first postwar Maserati, now under the Orsi-controlled Officine Alfieri Maserati S.p.A., was powered by a

variation of a supercharged twin-cam 6CM racing 6-cylinder engine conceived originally in 1936 by Ernesto Maserati. The final version was placed in the Maserati A6/1500 with a cubic capacity of 1488 to develop 65 braking horsepower at 4700 rpm through a 4-speed transmission. It could hit a top speed of 95 mph (152.8kph).

The A6/1500 was a roadable two-seater coupe that also came as a cabriolet. Pininfarina performed the coachbuilding tasks. It was an unusual offering for the Italian automaker, with its sleek, low design (only 47.2 inches [119.8cm] high), motorcycle-type fenders, sunroof, and disappearing headlamps. The front grille was square and split with small horizontal-bar intake units bisected by a vertical center bar and a pair of curved upper bars. The car was placed on a tubular chassis with a 100-inch (254cm) wheelbase.

Maserati followed with the A6G, similar to the A6 but with a larger, 1954-cc engine and leaf springs for rear suspension instead of coil springs. The A6G could now hit about 100 mph (160.9kph) and do 0–60 mph (0–96.5kph) in 12.5 seconds. The A6G enjoyed a production run from 1951

through 1957, but production figures are available only through 1954, with sixteen models produced.

In 1957, Maserati began building mass-produced cars in earnest. The first off the assembly floor was the 350GT. The 350GT kept the front end style of the A6G/2000 model, but the grille was recessed in an egg-crate style with the round trident insignia in the center. The 350GT featured auxiliary and parking lamps below the headlamps, a single chrome bumper, and an air scoop atop the hood. The roofline predated the attractive Mercedes-Benz two-door coupes, but the windshield and rear window were curved. Grille air intakes were placed on the cowls and above a single piece of chrome that ran from the front wheelwell to the rear.

Under the hood was a detuned 350S racing engine that displaced 3485 cc to generate 220 ponies at 5500 rpm. Torque was significant at 253 lbs.-ft. at 3500 rpm.

The 350GT, which debuted at the Geneva Salon in 1957, was offered as either a two-door 2-plus-2 coupe or the two-door Spider roadster. The roadster sold for the whopping price of $12,300, while the coupe went for slightly less ($11,400). Between 1957 and 1964, 2,223 350GTs were sold.

In 1962, the Sebring Series I 2-plus-2 notchback coupe replaced the 350GT with a modern body constructed by Vignale that sat atop a tubular-steel chassis with a 98-inch (248.9) wheelbase. Up until 1966, 444 Sebrings were produced at a price higher than that of the new 350GT Spider roadster.

The Mistral, which became available to buyers in 1963 and may be the last Maserati with a front-mounted inline 6-cylinder engine, enjoyed a reasonably long life, through 1970. It featured a 3485-cc aluminum block engine that developed 235 braking horsepower at 5800 rpm. In later versions, the cubic capacity was boosted to 3694 with pony power hiked to a whopping 255.

Yet the most enduring and perhaps the most popular Maserati off the showroom floor was the Mexico. Only 250 were produced from 1965 to 1968, but this two-door, four-passenger coupe offered the comfort of a sedan and the performance and handling of a serious street roadster. Its low belt line and profile on a rather large 103-inch (261.6cm) wheelbase gave the coupe the look of a stalking animal, hug-

of more than 155 mph (249.3kph) with 0–60 mph (0–96.5kph) performance at 7.5 seconds.

In 1968, Maserati joined Citroën in a partnership to develop a V6 engine. In 1971, the Citroën SM debuted. It was a handsome, high-performance vehicle with a 2670-cc aluminum block engine and a relatively high compression ratio of 9:1. It earned raves from the automotive press, with one journalist gushing that the Maserati/Citroën-powered SM "was like being in another world—a world of speed, comfort, and safety never felt before on any other car we have driven!"

In 1971, Maserati began using the mid-engine concept, developed by the firm's administrator, Guy Mallerat, in its new V6-powered Merak and the V8 Bora.

Abandoning the traditional front-engine design, Giorgetto Giugiaro styled the Bora with a short, flat, pointed nose, disappearing headlamps, and a near-horizontal fastback roofline. The Bora was also a product that displayed the new technological relationship between Maserati and Citroën, with high-pressure hydraulics operating the seat adjustments and brakes. The Bora sat on a 102-inch (259cm) wheelbase and was powered by a 4719-cc engine. The Merak adopted the Bora chassis and its V6 mid-engine.

There are few sports cars that so thoroughly blurred the lines between road car and race car as Maseratis. The most experienced owners often went to the trouble of tuning their Maseratis in an attempt to match street performance with successes on the track. Maserati's legacy is the impeccable standard it established that virtually all sports car makers follow today.

Maserati Merak SS (1980)

SPECIFICATIONS

Weight	3,185 lbs (1,445.9kg)
Tire size	185/70VR15 front, 205/70VR15
Engine type	90-degree dual-overhead-cam "vee" type 6-cylinder
Bore and Stroke	3.62 × 2.95 in.
Displacement	2965 cc
Compression ratio	8.5:1
Braking horsepower	220 @ 6500 rpm
Torque	199 lbs.-ft. at 4900 rpm
Transmission	5-speed manual
Carburetors	Three Weber carburetors

DIMENSIONS

Wheelbase	102.3 in. (259.8cm)
Length	181 in. (459.7cm)
Height	44.6 in. (113.2cm)
Width	69.6 in. (176.7cm)
Front tread	58 in. (147.3cm)
Rear tread	59.6 in. (151.3cm)

PERFORMANCE

0–60 mph (0–96.5kph)	N/A
Top speed	N/A

ging the ground as it approaches its prey. However, the Mexico's overall height of 53.2 inches (135.1cm) was not really that low. It featured a wide grille and hood with square rear-wheel openings, thin roof pillars, and unusually designed rear quarter panels in a pentagonal shape. Quad headlamps and horizontal taillamps were also featured with a Maserati script gracing the rear panel.

The 4136-cc V8 engine provided an 8.5:1 compression ration for 260 braking horsepower at 5000 rpm and breathed through four Weber carburetors. It could achieve a top speed

CHAPTER TWELVE

M G

There is probably no sports car that enthralled American motorists during the early postwar years more than the MG.

American servicemen stationed in England began a love affair with the little MG, renting or borrowing TA and TB sports roadsters to tool along the English countryside while on leave. When they returned stateside, many GIs brought their beloved MGs with them, and those who didn't created a huge market in the United States for the British roadster.

Despite a tight cockpit and relatively slow performance, the traditional-looking MG was probably the car most responsible for sparking an intense interest in European sports cars and road racing among Americans (with the possible exception of the Jaguar XK 120). Given its poor aerodynamics, the MG never did particularly well in professional road races, but it was affordable, good-looking, and fun to drive. Americans loved it.

MG stands simply for Morris Garages, the Oxford distributor for Morris cars, owned by William Morris. It was later purchased by Lord Nuffield, then went on to become a separate entity, Morris Motors.

The octagonal badge of MG began appearing on the first MG Special four-seater sports cars in 1924. By 1929, Morris Garages moved to Abingdon and was renamed M.G. Car Company, with the periods disappearing on American export models. During the first five years, the company topped the British racing circuit, winning the Brooklands 500, the Double-Twelve, and many Grand Prix events.

The famed T-Series sports cars debuted in spring 1936. The first one out of the gate was the TA, which incorporated the traditional MG design for its chassis with tubular crossmembers and front and rear leaf spring suspension. The hydraulic brakes were new to the TA. It was powered by what was to become a rather high-maintenance 1292-cc 4-cylinder engine that breathed through twin SU carburetors to produce 50 braking horsepower. The TA was a popular car

and did reasonably well in competition, but its engine had difficulty performing at high revs because of its poor valve timing and weak bottom end.

The TB Midget came out on the eve of World War II with essentially the same body and chassis but with a new and improved 1250-cc 4-cylinder engine.

The TC Midget made its first appearance at the 1945 London Motor Show and varied little from the TB, although it had a body that was 4 inches (10.1cm) wider and running boards that were slightly narrower. It was the TC that attracted wide attention from many American GIs who insisted on taking one home with them when they were discharged.

Although virtually all cars carried over a prewar design, the MG TC looked particularly dated, with its flimsy fenders and slab-sided fuel tank mounted on the rear. Sitting on a 94-inch (238.7cm) wheelbase, it was powered by a 1250-cc engine that generated 54 braking horsepower at 5200 rpm. It drove along nicely at 60 mph (96.5kph), but 75 mph (120.6kph) was really its top speed, and its acceleration was actually poorer than that of American-made offerings. The mechanicals and rather uncompromising interior also left a lot to be desired, but its romantic, striking lines and remarkable agility on the road made it an instant success. About ten thousand units were produced through 1949.

The TD Midget was introduced in late 1949. Created by stylist Cecil Cousins, it stood more upright but offered smoother lines. The TD was a product of the company's

insistence on a cheap and simple successor to the TC that could be produced quickly enough to meet the demand created by the TC models. That meant the TD still carried many of the characteristics of the TC, but offered many minor improvements. Gone were the front semielliptical leaf springs, which were replaced by an independent front suspension with twin control arms and coil springs.

As postwar demand increased, production leaped to 29,664 units during a four-year period before the TD Series II debuted in 1951. The Series II remained virtually unchanged in appearance from the original TD, but continued to improve with a more streamlined look.

New to the series was the TDC Mk II, a limited production model appearing in mid-1951. It featured an increased compression ratio of 8:1, with horsepower boosted first to 57, then later to 60. MG offered a dizzying number of engine tuning kits to boost speed. At the Bonneville Salt Flats in Utah, it did fairly well for its class, averaging 75.3 mph (121.2kph) over 12 hours.

PREVIOUS PAGE: The 1959 MG twin-cam coupe helped MG shed the shackles of prewar styling that had remained through the mid-1950s. By the dawn of the 1960s, there were several MGs to choose from, including the Mk I and Mk II models.

BELOW: The 1965 MG Midget demonstrates 1960s styling by eschewing the traditional, rounded form of the sports car. This style worked very well for MG with its sleek and uncluttered look. This version of the MG would last well into the 1970s.

While the styling of the MG was endearing and popular with American drivers, it was still archaic and needed a major face-lift. MG's reinterpretation came with the 1954 model year. The TF was sharper and lower, with the headlamps now integrated (with a bugeye look) into the fenders. Engine displacement remained the same at 1250 cc. While considered the most attractive of the T-Series models, the TF drew severe criticism from the automotive press for not moving forward enough in streamlining its design. And with the emergence of the much more powerful Triumph TR2, MG began losing ground with its American buyers.

The TF remained unchanged for 1955, but MG introduced the A Series 1500. This was a totally restyled car that incorporated modern lines long ago adopted by other British competitors, finally doing away with the traditional, stark, squarish look of the T Series. It now had an enclosed boot, a curved windshield, and an attractive fastback-style roofline.

Underneath it all was pretty much the old MG on the same 94-inch (238.7cm) wheelbase, although engine displacement jumped to 1489 cc to develop 68 braking horsepower at 5500 rpm.

The MGA now came as an envelope-bodied revolutionary coupe and roadster with low, sleek lines and an impressive array of gauges on the dash, including an enlarged speedometer and tachometer. Under the bonnet was a BMC 4-cylinder 1489-cc powerplant that offered a boosted 72 braking horsepower. With the additional ponies, it now could finally hit the magic 100 mph (160.9kph).

The MGA 1600 would follow with a new 1588-cc four-banger that gave 80 braking horsepower. Despite its continuing increase in power, its laggard time of 14.2 seconds for 0–60 mph (0–96.5kph) was still nothing to write home about. The 1600 also featured twin taillights and a small "1600" badge on the rear trunklid. The MGA remained in production through June 1962.

MG continued its tradition of providing inexpensive but fun cars. There was an enthusiastic market among the MG crowd that was attracted in the early 1960s to the MG Midget Mk I and II models. The Midget Mk I was a smaller version of the MGA, with a 1098-cc engine that developed 55 braking horsepower and had new standard disc brakes. By 1964, the semielliptic leaf springs were replaced with quarter-elliptic leaf springs to minimize the Midget's tendency to oversteer. The Mk II was offered until late 1965, when the Mk III was introduced with an enlarged 1275-cc engine.

ABOVE: This new generation MG is a 1996 model that reflects a slightly retro look from its MGA days, but is also not much different than other similar marques produced in its class.

Like every imported car in the late 1960s and early 1970s, MG was faced with stricter environmental and safety regulations. Many European marques had to quit exporting products to the United States because of prohibitive production costs. MG hung on longer than other British automakers, but it knew regulations would eventually bring about its downfall as MG committed itself to pouring in more resources to keep up with U.S. demands.

By 1975, MG debuted its final version of the Midget, the Mk IV, with a huge rubber nose replacing the former chromed grille. Made of soft black polyurethane, it was low with a wide opening, integrating the grille and bumper together. A similar but less massive black rubber bumper was fitted on the rear. It was hardly stylish, but MG's merger with British Leyland in the 1960s did result in other improvements. The MG now sported a Triumph Spitfire 1493-cc engine that featured a healthy 9.1:1 compression ratio and 55.5 braking horsepower at 5000 rpm. Its 0–60 mph (0–96.5kph) performance improved somewhat to 12.5 seconds. Still, American versions were slower, thanks to emissions demands from the U.S. government.

Midget production ceased in the summer of 1979. Production of the MGB ended in October 1980. The Midget had grown old gracefully since the original Mk I debuted and had evolved into a style that would remain contemporary for many years. The Mk III and Mk IV kept the basic body style for nearly two decades. Nearly 230,000 Midgets were produced, ensuring that collectors will have access to an adequate parts source network to keep MG cars on the road for years to come.

MG TD (1951)

SPECIFICATIONS

Weight —2,065 lbs. (929.3kg)	
Tire size —5.50 x 15	
Engine type —Inline, overhead-valve 4-cylinder	
Bore and stroke —2.62 x 3.54 in.	
Displacement —1250 cc	
Compression ratio —7.25:1	
Carburetor —Two SU	
Braking horsepower —54.4 @ 5200 rpm	
Torque —64 lbs.-ft. @ 2600 rpm	
Transmission —4-speed manual	

DIMENSIONS

Wheelbase —94 in. (238.7cm)	
Length —145 in. (368.3cm)	
Height —53 in. (134.6cm)	
Width —58.6 in. (148.8cm)	
Front tread —47.4 in. (120.3cm)	
Rear tread —50 in. (127cm)	

PERFORMANCE

0–60 mph (0–96.5kph) —23.5 seconds	
Top speed —80–83 mph (128.7–133.5kph)	

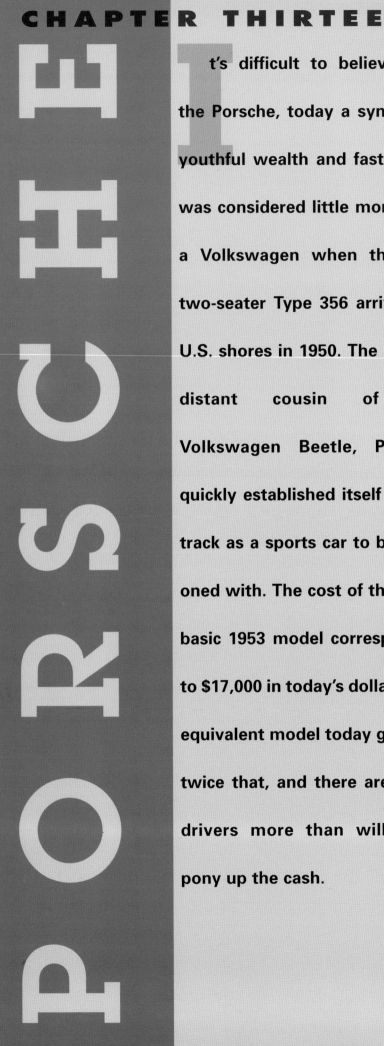

CHAPTER THIRTEEN

It's difficult to believe that the Porsche, today a symbol of youthful wealth and fast living, was considered little more than a Volkswagen when the first two-seater Type 356 arrived on U.S. shores in 1950. The not-so-distant cousin of the Volkswagen Beetle, Porsche quickly established itself on the track as a sports car to be reckoned with. The cost of the most basic 1953 model corresponded to $17,000 in today's dollars. The equivalent model today goes for twice that, and there are many drivers more than willing to pony up the cash.

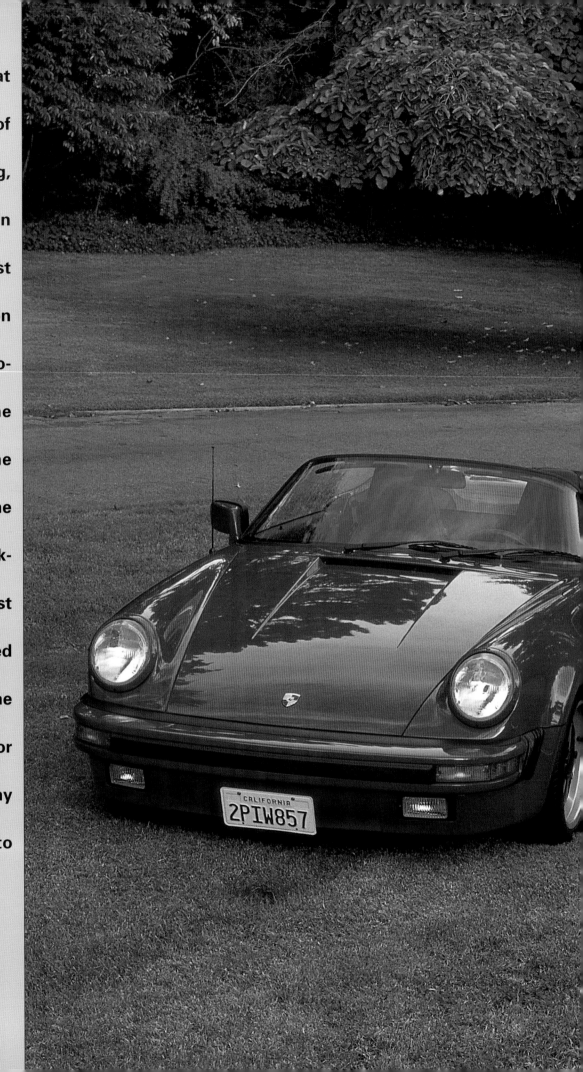

Its performance on the European racing circuit during the 1950s nudged the racing industry toward rear-engine technology. The 356's basic shape would endure through 1965, when the 912 Targa would debut and serve as the blueprint for Porsche design for the next three decades. And in an effort to return to its roots, the third-generation retro-style Boxster—which embodies some characteristics of the 356—was introduced in January 1997 as an answer to the BMW Z3 and Mercedes-Benz SLK230.

Porsche was the brainchild of Ferdinand Porsche, born in 1875, who worked in his family's metalsmith shop as a teenager and built a full electrical system for the family home when he was a young adult. With a strong interest in electricity and a natural aptitude for engineering, he developed an electric motor in 1897 that served as the foundation for many of his future inventions. He developed an electric car in 1900, then switched to aviation engines; in 1907, he designed the Austro-Daimler aviation engine.

As World War I was beginning to draw to a close, Porsche was named director of Austro-Daimler, and he designed a large 6-cylinder car. By 1923, as technical director at Austro-Daimler in Stuttgart, Germany, he built the super-charged Mercedes-Benz SS and SSK sports cars, both of which became premier road racers of the decade.

Porsche assembled a team of men who would set the stage for some of the most innovative rear-engine cars in the world. In 1930, he founded his own design firm in Stuttgart. Engineer Karl Rabe, another alumnus of Austro-Daimler, joined him and would remain as Porsche chief engineer into the mid-1960s. Porsche also recruited Joseph Kales, an expert in air-cooled engines, and designer Erwin Komenda. Rounding out the team was Porche's son, Ferdinand "Ferry" Porsche, Jr.

Adolf Hitler came to power in Germany in 1933 and a year later demanded that an inexpensive and reliable "people's car" be developed. Dubbed the Type 60, the Volkswagen beetle was born in 1936 amid much fanfare from the Nazi government and potential buyers. By September 1939, Porsche had a Volkswagen factory completed in Wolfsburg, but war put the Volkswagen on hold as Germany geared up for the fight.

After the war ended, Ferdinand and his son were arrested by American occupation forces. Ferry was freed in 1946, but his father remained imprisoned for another year. Upon Ferry's release, he was ordered by French authorities to build the Renault 4CV.

The 356 built by Ferry and Ferdinand Porsche in 1948 was based mostly on Volkswagen components, although it did feature a tubular space frame on an 87.7-inch (222.7cm) wheelbase. Ferdinand was named design consultant for Volkswagen in late 1948, making the connection between the two marques very close.

Initial prototypes had the rear engine ahead of the rear wheels, but it was later moved further back. The 356 was an excellent aerodynamic model, with rounded front and rear fenders and a sloping nose. Headlamps were integrated into the front fenders, while the front bumper was molded into and painted the same color as the body. The 356 featured a split windshield that would disappear by 1954. It also possessed some of the maddening features of a Volkswagen. While an oil gauge was added, the 356 had no fuel gauge, requiring owners to use a dipstick to measure the level of gasoline or rely on the 1-gallon (3.7L) reserve fuel tank not to run out of gas.

Initial models offered a 1086-cc engine with a 7:1 compression ratio to generate 40 horsepower at 4200 rpm, a considerable boost from the standard Volkswagen engine of the time.

Manufactured in Gmund, Austria, and later in Stuttgart, the first 356 models were imported to the United States in 1950. The 356 entered its first race at Le Mans in 1950 and finished twelfth, although it would perform better at other European races and win its class at Le Mans the following year. It was the last achievement Ferdinand Porsche would see. He died in 1951.

While Porsche would boost its engine displacement to 1286 and 1488 cc in some models, U.S. importer Max Hoffman, the primary importer of Porsches, stopped accepting 1.1- and 1.3-liter models because they wouldn't satisfy the power needs of American buyers. Only the 1488-cc models were available in the United States during this period.

The Speedster was offered to the public in September 1954. A roadster version of earlier models, it weighed only 1,675 pounds (760.4kg) and featured a chopped one-piece windshield that was more than 3 inches (7.6cm) lower than

the regular model. The 1.5-liter Speedster could hit 60 mph (96.5kph) in 14.7 seconds, a respectable achievement for its output. The Super Speedster, which offered the same cubic capacity but had a 8.2:1 compression ratio and 70 horsepower, could reach 60 mph (96.5kph) in 10 seconds.

By the end of the 1950s, more than twenty-five thousand Porsche 356 models were on the road worldwide.

Ferdinand Alexander Porsche, eldest son of Ferry Porsche, was designing a new body in 1961 that would accommodate a new 6-cylinder engine. It wouldn't appear until the debut of the 2-liter 911 A Series in July 1965. The 911 was the successor to the 356 models, with a horizontally

opposed, air-cooled engine that offered a 9:1 compression ratio to generate 130 horsepower at 6100 rpm. Its 0–60 mph (0–96.5kph) performance was Porsche's best ever at a flat 8 seconds with a top speed of 130 mph (209.1kph).

Ferdinand Alexander Porsche's new design featured a body on a wheelbase 4.4 inches (11.1cm) longer than the 356 and 6 inches (15.2cm) longer overall. While styling embodied many of the characteristics of the 356, the rear was now fashioned into a fastback with the front slicing to the nose in a "knife-edged" appearance.

In 1968, Porsche won a succession of European races that enhanced its reputation for speed, durability, and superb

handling. It captured first-place honors at the Targa Florio, the Sebring 12-hour marathon, and the Rallye Monte Carlo.

Two years later, Porsche debuted an all-new model, the 914, to replace the short-lived 912 that was produced from 1965 to 1969. Like the early 356s, the 914 used many Volkswagen components, particularly the all-Volkswagen 1679-cc 4-cylinder engine. The optional Porsche-built engine was a 2-liter flat 6-cylinder. The 914 was received as something of an odd duck in racing circles with its squarish body design and mid-engine placement. The 914 would remain in production until the 1977 model year, when it was replaced by the 924.

In 1976, the Turbo Carrera was a monster success, exceeding all expectations in the sports car market. It achieved top status as the fastest Porsche ever, with a 3-liter flat-six engine that could develop 234 horsepower to hit 60 mph (96.5kph) in only 4.9 seconds and a top speed of 156 mph (251kph). All this for U.S. imports! Featuring the easily identifiable "whale tail" spoiler on the rear, its wheelwells were flared to accommodate extra-wide tires on cast-aluminum wheels. About fourteen hundred Turbo Carreras were produced during its initial run.

The 911 Targa also achieved top status as Porsche's reigning model since 1965. In 1996, the 911 Targa Carrera was the cream of the crop in street Porsches. In that year, a glass-top 911 Targa Carrera appeared, featuring a fully retracting glass roof in which the entire area over the passenger compartment slides under the rear window. It's the greenhouse look first introduced by Ford on its Crown Victorias in the mid-1950s but with 1990s technology to provide privacy and sun blockage and to keep out ultraviolet rays.

The Targa Carrera is powered by a 3.6-liter all-aluminum air-cooled 6-cylinder engine that delivers 282 horsepower at 6300 rpm and 250 lbs.-ft. of torque at 5250 rpm. With a Digital Motor Electronic fuel injection and dual ignition system, the Targa Carrera could get its driver to 60

The 1966 Porsche 906 racing car was unlike any other Porsche on or off the racing track. It stunned the racing motor world with its full-throttle fury and superb handling.

mph (96.5kph) from a standstill in 5.3 seconds and cover the quarter mile (402.3m) in 14.2 seconds.

The first all-new Porsche in nineteen years debuted in 1997. The Boxster, named for its horizontally opposed "boxer" engine and roadster chassis, was first displayed as a concept car at the 1993 Detroit Auto Show. The Boxster was designed in an effort to harken back to Porsche's sports car heritage with its open cockpit and resemblance to 356 lines. Abandoning its traditional air-cooled technology, the Boxster features a water-cooled 2.5-liter mid-engine 6-cylinder engine to develop 204 horsepower with a top speed of 149 mph (239.7kph) and 0–60 mph (0–96.5kph) in 6.9 seconds.

OPPOSITE: Sporting a new style, the 1997 Porsche Turbo S kept many of its predecessor's styling characteristics but offering a softer, more streamlined look.

BELOW: Continuing to maintain a racing tradition, the 1988 Porsche 959S did exceptionally well against the likes of Maserati and Ferrari during the 1980s.

Employing racing technology, the engine power is transmitted to the rear wheels either through a 5-speed manual tranny or the optional Tiptronic S automatic system. The new Tiptronic transmission uses five forward gears instead of four as in the previous Tiptronic version. The four disc brakes are inner-vented, while all four brake calipers are equipped with four pistons of varying diameters to avoid uneven wear on the brake linings.

The Boxster won the 1997 *MotorWeek* Drivers' Choice Award for Best Sports Car. It's the least expensive of the Porsche offerings with a price tag beginning at $39,980, but it still plays in a different league than the BMW Z3 and the Mercedes-Benz SLK. Unlike the 914 of the '70s and the 924 (a water-cooled front-engine model using some Volkswagen components) and 944 (an evolution of the 924) of the '80s, the Boxster is more expensive as an entry-level model and is really geared to current Porsche drivers looking for a replacement for their 911s rather than to new buyers.

In 1983, Porsche began building a fierce super sports car, the Type 959. Three years later, three 959s, with electronically controlled all-wheel drive, finished first, second, and sixth at the Rallye Paris. And a Porsche-powered Formula One McLaren single-seater captured three World Championships in a row. At the 1991 Le Mans, Porsche captured another first place to duplicate its first victory at the French race forty years earlier.

With its continuing successes on the track and its commitment to innovative designs and engine technology, Porsche is perhaps the most popular and successful imported sports car on American shores.

Porsche Turbo Carrera (1977)

SPECIFICATIONS

Weight—2,490 lbs. (1,130.4kg)

Tire size—225/50VR16

Engine type—Horizontally opposed, overhead-cam 6-cylinder

Bore and stroke—3.74 x 2.76 in.

Displacement—2993 cc

Compression ratio—6.5:1

Braking horsepower—234 @ 5500 rpm

Torque—245 lbs.-ft. @ 4000 rpm

Transmission—Wide-ratio 4-speed manual

Fuel injection—Bosch K-Jetronic

DIMENSIONS

Wheelbase—89.4 in. (227cm)

Length—168.9 in. (429cm)

Height—52 in. (132cm)

Width—69.9 in. (177.5cm)

Front tread—56.4 in. (143.2cm)

Rear tread—59.1 in. (150.1cm)

PERFORMANCE

0–60 mph (0–96.5kph)—4.9 seconds

Quarter mile (402.3m)—13.5 seconds

Top speed—156 mph (251kph)

CHAPTER FOURTEEN

TRIUMPH

Its low-cut doors, high-standing headlamps, and surging power in the early postwar years made Triumph one of the most desirable sports cars in the United States, next to Jaguar and MG. And nearly every Triumph owner will tell you that not only did the Triumph TR2 and TR3 outperform the MG, its closest competitor, but it also outsold MG overall.

Triumph was a masculine sports car, but very unlike Ferrari or Jaguar, given the fact that many of its models through the years offered little in the way of lasting comfort. Often cramped and providing little protection from the weather with its ragtops, many models had a rough ride. Only the hardy need apply for the long drive.

But that was part of the mystique of the Triumph as it grew in popularity with each passing year.

Triumph started first as a bicycle-building company in 1887 before turning to motorcycles and three-wheeled vehicles at the turn of the century. In 1923, Triumph tackled a four-wheeled version in the form of a 1.4-liter 4-cylinder engine with a 4-speed gearbox. As the company grew and began to focus on motorcars, it changed its name in 1930 from Triumph Cycle Co. Ltd. to Triumph Motor Co. Ltd. It developed the 6-cylinder Scorpion a year later and put Coventry Climax engines into its Super Nine models.

By the end of the decade, Triumph fell into receivership and after World War II, became a subsidiary of the Standard Motor Co. in Canley, England.

An early effort after the war and the vehicle most responsible for sending Triumph into the sports car market was the 1800 sports roadster, introduced in 1946 and produced through 1948. Sitting on a 100-inch (254cm) wheelbase, it was a majestic piece of machinery with overwhelming pontoon fenders, separately mounted headlamps, and a tall, angled vertical-bar grille. It was powered by a 1776-cc 4-cylinder engine with 65 horsepower. It claimed a top speed of 84 mph (135.1kph), although 0–50 mph (80.4kph) clocking was a disappointing 16 seconds. An estimated 2,501 units were produced, with about 750 earmarked for export.

The 1800 was replaced by the 2000, a 2-liter version that retained many of the characteristics of the older model. Although the 1800 and 2000 were fine motorcars, Triumph didn't make a serious attempt at capturing the American market until its introduction in 1954 of the TR2, its first real postwar sports car, which kicked off the TR Series and lasted until 1981.

The TR2 was by far the most easily identifiable sports car on the road after the MG. It was born after Sir John Black, head of Standard Motors, visited the United States and returned determined to target the American market. He wanted a cheap but quick and nimble car.

Black's first effort was the TR1 with 75 braking horsepower, but it was later modified during a year's worth of developmental work. Born from the TR1 was the TR2 with its doors cut down considerably and the grille deeply recessed and featuring an egg-crate pattern. Its bulging headlamps were integrated on the front fenders and the wheelwells were fully rounded. Under the bonnet was a 1991-cc 4-cylinder engine with 90 horsepower and the ability to hit a top speed of about 103 mph (165.7kph). It outperformed the MG with its superior power output and exceptional handling. Sales mushroomed to 8,636 units with a whopping 5,521 TR2s sold for export. Production of the TR2 started in August 1953 and ended in October 1955.

The TR2 evolved into the TR3 with the same cubic capacity, but with a boosted braking horsepower and better top speed. It proved itself admirably by finishing its first Le Mans event, capturing top awards in the Tourist Trophy and the Alpine Rally Team Prize, and finishing seventh in its class at Mille Miglia.

Introduced at the 1955 London Motor Show, the TR3 included a new "surface" grille that was actually mounted over the old one. There was an occasional seat installed in the back for tiny children. Under the bonnet were new and bigger SU carburetors to increase power output to 100 braking horsepower. Top speed now reached 107 mph (160.9kph). Drum brakes were used on most units through the production run, which ended in September 1956, but disc brakes were added as standard equipment toward the end of the run.

In the early and mid-1960s, Triumph offered a variety of sports cars to satisfy the growing market of small-car buyers created by MG and Austin-Healey. Triumph now offered the Spitfire Mk I and II, the TR3B, and the TR4, all 4-cylinder models. The Spitfire was in response to the MG Midget and Austin-Healey's Sprite. Designed by Italy's Giovanni Michelotti, the Spitfire featured a small split grille, partially recessed headlamps, and doors that were just slightly cut down compared to the TR3 models. Built with welded monocoque construction, it sat on a very short 83-inch (210.8cm) wheelbase. Its front fenders and bonnet tilted upward for full access to the engine.

The Mk I and Mk II Spitfires weighed only 1,474 pounds (669.1kg) each and sold at a very reasonable price, ranging from $2,155 to $2,300. Sales skyrocketed to 45,753 for the Mk I production run from 1962 to 1964 and 37,409 for the Mk II run from 1964 to 1967.

TR3Bs did not do well in the United States, but the TR4, a "full-size" sports car also styled by Michelotti, sold more than forty thousand units between 1961 and 1964. The TR4 differed greatly from the TR3, with rack and pinion steering and a longer, lower, wider look.

Power for the Spitfires came from a 1147-cc four-banger generating 63 and 67 horsepower for the Mk I and Mk II, respectively. Later the TR3B and TR4 offered 2138-cc engines with horsepower measured at 100.

PREVIOUS PAGES: The 1948 1800 Triumph roadster sat on a 100-inch (254cm) wheelbase and was powered by a 1776-cc 4-cylinder engine. Only thirty-one were sold in the United States in 1948.

LEFT: The 1967 Triumph Mk I wasn't much to look at and didn't represent the best in Triumph technology and performance. Production, however, was strong enough to keep Triumph afloat as it struggled with tighter U.S. regulations on automotive safety.

By February 8, 1968, more than 100,000 Spitfires had been produced, with three out of four being exported and half of the exports going to the United States.

The Mk III was livelier than its predecessors, with a 1296-cc engine, road performance of 0–60 mph (0–96.5kph) in about 14.5 seconds, and a top speed of 95 mph (152.8kph). The 1500 version that was introduced later hit 60 mph (96.5kph) in 11.8 seconds and could hit nearly 100 mph (160.9kph) if babied right. These cars performed well enough, but poor heating and ventilation and a rough ride with subpar suspension didn't make them good cars for the faint of heart.

The Mk IV and 1500 models represented remarkable improvements in handling and overall performance in the Spitfire. But one has to wonder what British Leyland, the new owner of Triumph, was thinking when it produced the Spitfire with such questionable chassis components, particularly in the rear. Even attempting to achieve 100 mph (160.9kph) in an early Spitfire was risky business.

The front consisted of unequal-length wishbones and coil springs, but the rear had the arcane transverse leaf springs with the old-style swing axles. The design made handling in the rear outright dangerous. Professional testers and Triumph sales personnel even warned prospective owners to take care when driving at high speeds. The consensus among owners today is that body styling took precedence over chassis and suspension design with a larger-than-usual luggage compartment for a sports car.

The TR6 enjoyed a long run, from 1968 to 1976, with styling continuing the TR Series theme. A flatter hood, wider blackout grille, and chopped-off tail were significant in the new body design. Europeans enjoyed fuel-injected models, while Americans received carbureted versions with much less power. There were few changes over the years, although many minor improvements were made. Initial TR6s featured a 2498-cc 6-cylinder engine with an 8.6:1 compression ratio and 104 ponies. For the 1972–73 models, compression was dropped to 7.75:1 compression ratio but the horsepower was boosted slightly to 106.

British Leyland billed the TR7 as "the shape of things to come." It certainly was a bold move, although it wasn't necessarily a harbinger of the future. The TR7 followed a

long line of handsome sports cars, but enthusiasts couldn't figure out for the life of them the continuity of this model from the previous ones. It was nothing like any TR Series sports car.

British Leyland, which was in dire financial straits in the late 1970s, was faced with disturbing news from the United States. Pending legislation would ban convertible cars and require bumpers to withstand a 5 mph (8kph) crash in which the body would not be damaged and the bumper would be able to pop back into place. Accordingly, the TR7 was designed to meet these new regulations, but Leyland miscalculated. Convertibles were not banned as expected and the 5 mph (8kph) bumper crash requirement was reduced to 2.5 mph (4kph).

The Triumph TR6, this one a 1974 model, sported a flatter bonnet and headlamps repositioned farther out front. The boot features a chopped off tail. The TR6 debuted in 1969, and was produced through model year 1976.

The principal designer of the TR7 was Harris Mann, an alumnus of the old Austin-Morris design studios. British Leyland's "shape of things to come" was the Wedge. It was extremely low in the front, almost knifelike in appearance, with a high tail and wide overall look. It looked very much like a big wedge of cheese. It had an 85-inch (215.9cm) wheelbase and weighed 5,100 pounds (2,315.4kg)—by no means light—and was powered by a 1998-cc 4-cylinder engine with a paltry 85 to 90 horses.

If the styling wasn't questionable enough, British Leyland was experiencing its most difficult internal struggles in the history of its operation. The entire British automobile industry in the mid-1970s was experiencing strikes, and sabotage of cars was a common problem. British Leyland was in the thick of it with its Speke factory in the middle of some very ugly labor problems. British Leyland finally closed the troubled operation in 1978 after a particularly troubling strike in October 1977 during which very few 1978 TR7s were produced.

These problems coupled with the new look of the TR7 did little to inspire buyer confidence. Between 1975 and 1981 about 112,368 units were produced. That wasn't a bad number, but it was far below expectations.

The making of the TR8 was British Leyland's last gasp to recoup lost sales of the TR7. It was basically a 3528-cc V8 engine, which once powered compact General Motors cars in the United States, crammed into a TR7 body. Only 2,497 were produced before Triumph permanently shut down in October 1981.

Despite its inglorious demise, Triumph still conjures the image of swift handling and sensual power in a cheap but very satisfying sports car.

ABOVE: Perhaps the TR8 could be called the "Big Cheese" with its radical wedge-shaped body. Triumph owners were puzzled over the lack of continuity from the TR6 to the TR7 and TR8. By 1981, Triumph was already dying as a car maker.

Triumph TR3A Roadster (1959)

SPECIFICATIONS

Weight —2,016 pounds (915.2kg)

Tire size —5.50 X 15

Engine —Inline, overhead-valve, 4-cylinder

Bore and stroke —3.27 x 3.62 in.

Displacement —1991 cc

Compression ratio —8.5:1

Carburetor —Two SU

Braking horsepower —100 @ 5000 rpm

Torque —117 lbs.- ft. @300 rpm

Transmission —4-speed manual

DIMENSIONS

Wheelbase —88 in. (223.5cm)

Length —151 in. (383.5cm)

Height —50 in. (127cm)

Width —55.5 in. (140.9cm)

Front tread —45 in. (114.3cm)

Rear tread —45.5 in. (115.5cm)

PERFORMANCE

0–60 mph (0–96.5 kph) —12.5 seconds

Top speed —102 mph (164.1 kph)

GLOSSARY

ABS BRAKES: Antilock Braking System, which provides skid-free braking under poor traction conditions by preventing brakes from locking and allowing the vehicle to be steered while the driver is braking.

AC: A common abbreviation for Auto Carrier, an English automaker known for its dramatic sports cars in the 1950s and 1960s who later supplied chassis and bodies to Carroll Shelby for the famed Cobras.

ACTIVE SUSPENSION: A computer-controlled system of hydraulic rams and valves that replaces springs and shock absorbers.

ALFETTA: Perhaps the most famous Alfa Romeo race car of the early 1950s. The Alfetta raced in eleven Grand Prix races and won every one of them

ANTI-LIFT: A suspension system that minimizes body lift during extreme acceleration or jacking under braking.

BACKBONE CHASSIS: A form of aerospace monocoque chassis first developed by Lotus for passenger car use.

BLOWN: Provided with a supercharged engine.

BLUEPRINTING: A careful match of intake and exhaust ports and cylinder capacities to ensure maximum efficiency of airflow through the engine.

BONNET: A British term for the engine hood.

BOOT: A British term for the trunk of a car.

BUGEYE: A term for protruding headlamps on the bonnet, such as on the Austin-Healey two-seater Sprite sports car from 1958 to 1961.

CAMBER: The angle of the wheel as measured from the vertical plane. A wheel with the top tilted inward has a negative camber; a wheel tilted outward has a positive camber.

CASTER: The angle of the inclination of a wheel's steering axis.

CHASSIS: The frame of a car to which the suspension, drivetrain, and bodywork are attached.

COIL SPRING: A heavy wire coil that holds the car off the suspension.

COMPOSITE: A combination of materials used for a car body.

COUPE: A two-door vehicle with a fixed roof.

CUBIC CAPACITY: A measure of displacement of the engine, generally used by European auto and truck makers.

CUBIC INCHES: An American measure of displacement of the engine.

DINO: The name of a Ferrari model. It was named after Enzo Ferrari's son, who died in 1956.

DIRECT IGNITION: An electronic ignition in which the ignition coil fires directly into the spark plugs.

DOUBLE OVERHEAD CAM: A pair of rotating shafts in the cylinder head in which an engine's contours, or lobs, bring about the opening of its intake and exhaust valves at the top of the combustion chamber.

DROPHEAD COUPE: A British term for a convertible.

EARL'S COURT MOTOR SHOW: A popular annual British auto show in London where new cars are debuted.

FIXED HEAD: A British term for a solid, nonremovable roof.

FORMULA CAR: An open-wheeled, single-seat race car.

FORMULA ONE: An international racing series considered the pinnacle of motor racing.

FROGEYE: See **Bugeye**.

FRONT ENGINE: The traditional location of an engine at the front of the automobile over the front wheels. Racing vehicles began abandoning front-engine cars about 1960 in favor of rear- and mid-engine designs.

FUEL INJECTION: The distribution of fuel into the engine's combustion chambers via injection.

GENEVA AUTO SHOW: Switzerland's annual auto show.

GROUND EFFECTS: A term first coined by Lotus founder Colin Chapman for the use of airflow beneath the Lotus Formula One race car in 1978. The car used an undertray to produce vast amounts of downpressure, or vacuum, that held the car down on the pavement to enhance cornering and handling ability.

GULLWING: A term used for the Mercedes-Benz 300SL Gullwing coupe, on which the doors were hinged on the roof to open upward. The Gullwing coupe was produced from 1954 to1957.

HEADLAMP: A British term for a headlight.

HOOD: A British term for a convertible top.

KEVLAR: An advanced fiber made of aramid that has ten times the tensile strength of steel.

KPH: Kilometers per hour.

LE MANS: The French 24-hour Grand Prix.

LIGHT: A British term for a window.

MID-ENGINE: An engine located between the front and rear wheels.

MONOCOQUE: A structure where the outer skin carries all or the majority of the load. Modified monocoques are used in most cars today and are called unit body or unibody.

MPH: Miles per hour.

OIL COOLER: A radiator that cools engine or transmission oil.

OVERSTEER: A condition in which the rear tires of a car are more prone to slide than the front tires.

PININFARINA: Italy's most revered coachbuilder. The family-owned operation designed and built some of world's finest body styles, including Ferrari and Maserati. Also spelled Pinin Farina.

RACK AND PINION: A steering system in which the steering wheel shaft rotates a gear called the pinion and the rack, a cogged bar, is engaged with the pinion. It allows for very little play in the steering wheel.

REAR ENGINE: An engine mounted at the rear of an automobile above the rear wheels.

REVERSE LOCK: A steering technique in which the front wheels are pointed in the opposite direction of the turn. This technique can prevent spinouts.

SALOON: A British term for a sedan.

SEBRING: The 12-hour marathon race held at Sebring, Florida.

SHOCK ABSORBER: A twin-tube hydraulic unit that dampens the movement of the car body and suspension components.

SPORTS CAR: An aerodynamically shaped automobile that has a low center of gravity and is designed to provide precise control in steering and suspension at high speeds.

SPORTS RACER: A two-seater enclosed race car.

TESTAROSSA: Literally translated, this wildly popular Ferrari model means "redhead." Also spelled Testa Rossa.

TUBULAR CHASSIS: A chassis constructed of tubing, usually steel, to save weight. Tube chassis were often 3 or 4 inches (7.6 or 10.1cm) in diameter.

TURIN AUTO SHOW: Italy's annual auto show famous for debuting the top luxury cars of the world.

UNBLOWN: Not equipped with a supercharged engine.

WHEELBASE: The measure of the chassis between the center of the front and rear wheels.

XKE: Jaguar's E-Type sports car, dubbed the XKE in the United States. Production of the XKE ran from 1961 to 1974.

BIBLIOGRAPHY

Automobile Quarterly, vol. 15, no. 3, Third Quarter 1977.

Bennett, Frank H. "The Cobra Strikes Again." *Road & Track*, October 1963.

Borgeson, Griffith, and Eugene Jaderquist. *Sports and Classic Cars*. Englewood Cliffs, N.J.: Prentice Hall, Inc., 1955.

Browning, Peter, and John Blunsden. *The Jensen Healey Stories*. Croydon, Surrey, England: Motor Racing Publications, 1974.

Clarke, R.M., comp. *Alfa Romeo Spider, 1966–1990*. Brooklands Book Distribution Ltd., 1991.

Clymer, Floyd. *Treasury of Foreign Cars Old and New*. New York: McGraw-Hill, 1957.

Crow, James T. "Cobra Wins Le Championnat des Constructeurs." *Road & Track*, October 1965.

Dammann, George H. *75 Years of Chevrolet*. Sarasota, Fla.: Crestline Publishing, 1986.

Flammang, James M., ed. *Standard Catalog of Imported Cars, 1946–1990*. Iola, Wis.: Krause Publications, Inc., 1994.

Fox, Charles. *The Great Racing Cars and Drivers*. New York: Grosset & Dunlap, Inc., 1972.

General Motors Public Relations Department/Chevrolet Communications. Various press releases.

Gunnell, John, ed. *Standard Catalog of American Cars, 1946–1975*. Iola, Wis.: Krause Publications, Inc., 1992.

Kramer, Ralph. "The Leader, the Legend: A Tribute to the Life and Times of Corvette Superstar Zora Arkus-Duntov." *Corvette Fever*, August 1996.

Ludvigsen, Karl. "Test of the TR3." *Sports Cars Illustrated*, August 1956.

Lurani, Giovanni. *History of the Racing Car: Man and Machine*. Thomas Y. Crowell Co., 1972.

Pritchard, Anthony. *Lotus: The Sports Racing Cars*. Wellingborough, England: Patrick Stephens Ltd., 1987.

Stein, Ralph. *The Greatest Cars*. New York: Simon and Schuster, 1979.

PHOTO CREDITS

INDEX